THE UNIVERSITY OF
KENTUCKY

THE UNIVERSITY OF
KENTUCKY
A Pictorial History

■

Carl B. Cone

THE UNIVERSITY PRESS OF KENTUCKY

To the thousands of students through the years
who loved the university and went from it
to reflect credit upon their alma mater

Frontispiece: Portion of a painting of State
University of Kentucky by Arthur J. Elder.

Copyright © 1989 by The University Press of Kentucky

Scholarly publisher for the Commonwealth,
serving Bellarmine College, Berea College, Centre
College of Kentucky, Eastern Kentucky University,
The Filson Club, Georgetown College, Kentucky
Historical Society, Kentucky State University,
Morehead State University, Murray State University,
Northern Kentucky University, Transylvania University,
University of Kentucky, University of Louisville,
and Western Kentucky University.

Editorial and Sales Offices: Lexington, Kentucky 40506-0336

Library of Congress Cataloging-in-Publication Data

Cone, Carl B.
    The University of Kentucky: a pictorial history / Carl B. Cone.
        p.   cm.
    ISBN 0-8131-1696-1
    1. University of Kentucky—History.   2. University of Kentucky
—History—Pictorial works.   I. Title.
LD2773.C66   1990
378.769'47'09—dc20   89-36823

This book is printed on acid-free paper meeting
the requirements of the American National Standard
for Permanence of Paper for Printed Library Materials.
∞

Contents

PHOTO CREDITS

Most photographs in this book were from collections housed in the University Archives in the Department of Special Collections and Archives, Margaret I. King Library. Photos were also received from the following university collections and files: Alumni Association; College of Arts and Sciences; College of Home Economics; College of Pharmacy; Department of Physics; Department of Agricultural Communications; Department of Communications; Donovan Program; Medical Center Archives; Music Department; Office of Minority Student Affairs; Patterson School of Diplomacy and International Commerce; Photographic Services; Singletary Center for the Arts, Art Museum; Sports Information Department; and University Information Services.

In addition, individual photos are courtesy of :
Kentucky Department of Arts, p. 214 bottom, p. 215
Lexington Herald-Leader, staff, pp. 122, 124 top, 154, 161; David Perry, p. 222; David Sterling, p. 229 bottom
Louisville Courier-Journal, p. 210 right; Bill Strode, p. 209 bottom left
Transylvania University Library, J. Winston Coleman Kentuckiana Collection, pp. 31, 81, 82
Wendell Berry, p. 211 bottom left
Clyde T. Burke, p. 201 top
Wendell Cherry, p. 216 top
David Coyle, p. 36 left and center
James F. Gordon, p. 209 bottom left
Harlan H. Grooms, p. 209 bottom right
Host Communications, Thomas F. Maguire, Jr., p. 236
Walter D. Huddleston, p. 214 top left
The Kentucky Architect, p. 149
Mrs. Elizabeth Kirwan, p. 160
Tony Leonard, p. 140
Carol Lotz, p. 219
Mitch McConnell, p. 214 top right
Jack Parker, p. 212 top
J.W. Patterson, p. 224 top
Chuck Perry, pp. 174 bottom, 175 top, 191 left, 194 bottom, 197 right, 198 bottom, 199 bottom, 224 bottom, 225 top, 226 bottom, 227 top left, 228 top
Scott Reed, p. 209 top
Donald Webb, p. 216 bottom left and right
Henry R. Wilhoit, p. 209 bottom center
Thomas Victor, p. 211 bottom right

For the photographic record of the university's early years, Louis E. Nollau deserves special mention. While serving as professor of engineering drawing (1904-1953), he took thousands of pictures—of State College, State University, and the University of Kentucky. His nitrate negatives in the Photographic Archives, well represented in this book, greatly enrich our picture of UK's past. Nollau died in 1955.

Preface

A pictorial history combines the virtues of words and pictures. Together they tell the history of the University of Kentucky more vividly than words alone and more informatively than pictures alone.

The Special Collections Department in the University of Kentucky's Margaret I. King Library, and within it the University Archives and the Photographic Archives, supplied most of my research needs. William Marshall, assistant director of libraries for Special Collections, and Frank B. Stanger, assistant archivist and curator of the Photographic Archives, were especially helpful. Director Marshall gave me free run of Special Collections, and Frank Stanger knew where everything was that I wanted, made it accessible to me, and cooperated with the staff of the University Press to make it available for their purposes.

It hardly needs saying but should nevertheless be said that my searches in the library, elsewhere in the university, and outside it were made pleasant and fruitful by the unfailing courtesy and interest of the people, named below, who provided material, information, and services.

The following submitted to interviews or formal discussions: Frank G. Dickey and Otis A. Singletary, former presidents of the university; Lewis W. Cochran, former Vice-President for Academic Affairs; Don Sands, Vice Chancellor for Academic Affairs of the Lexington Campus; Lucy Hogan and Anne L. Wilson, former presidential secretaries; the late Helen King, first director of the Alumni Association; and Sallie Pence, who taught mathematics before and after World War II. (Miss Pence is the daughter of the first head of the department of physics, Merry L. Pence, who was also a student on the old Woodlands campus. Father and daughter, they span all but the first fifteen and the last few years of the university's history.)

Within the university, I received help from many people: Art Gallaher, chancellor, Lexington campus; Wimberly Royster, vice-president for Research and Graduate Studies; Dan Reedy, associate dean for Graduate Studies; Jane Cunningham, Harriett E. McVey, and Paul Owens of University Relations; John R. Mitchell, Emily J. Maggard, and Joyce A. Moore of Photographic Services; Mary Margaret Colliver of Public Affairs, Medical Center; Jay Brumfield, secretary and director of the Alumni Association; Paul Sears, professor of chemistry and assistant to the president; Mike Kenny, formerly of the Registrar's Office; Dan Tudor of the central office of the Community College System; James Y. McDonald of the UK Research Foundation; Joan McCauley of the Planning and Budget Office;

Robert R. Marshall of the Controller's Office; Paula Anderson, formerly of Student Publications; Carol Lotz and David Elbon of the Computing Center; the Athletic Association Public Information Office; Terry Mobley and Rex Bailey of the Development Office; Clifford Long and Jennifer Krieger of the UK Police Department; Harry Gilbert, former librarian, College of Architecture; Cecil D. Garrett of the physics department; Professor Vincent Davis and Darlene E. Mickey of the Patterson School of Diplomacy; Roberta James of the Council on Aging; J.G. Duncan, formerly of Public Information, College of Agriculture; Terry L. Birdwhistell, university archivist and director of Oral History; Chester Grundy, director, Minority Student Affairs; William J. Hennessey, director, Art Museum; Sarah Henry, assistant dean, College of Home Economics; Doris A. McKay, College of Pharmacy; Carolyn Willhoit, Agricultural Communication; Lee E. Marcum and Mary H. Smith, department of music; Professor Emeritus Clifford Blyton and Professor J.W. Patterson of Communications; and Clifford Amyx, professor of art, emeritus. Dr. Charles G. Talbert, associate professor of history, retired, was a valuable resource person on matters pertaining to the history of the university.

Seeking pictures outside the university, I turned to the late Maurice Strider, artist and photographer; Judge Henry R. Wilhoit, Jr.; Bruce T. Bell, attorney; Jack Parker; C. Thomas Hardin, director of photography, the Louisville *Courier-Journal*; Jim Jennings, department of photography, the Lexington *Herald-Leader*; the photography department of the Kentucky Department of the Arts; F.A.C. Thompson, '23, of Fulton County, who gave to the university his collection of photographs taken when he was an engineering student; Bennett H. Wall, professor of history, emeritus, University of Georgia; Betty Kirwan, widow of the university's seventh president; Sarah McInteer Belker of New York City; Mrs. Frank Lockridge of Tucson; Chuck Perry, a former history graduate student and a photographer; and Rush Mathews, Jr., photographer. John Ed Pearce, formerly of the *Courier-Journal*, shared his knowledge of between-the-wars campus humor magazines.

In casual conversations, many people provided information or clarification about recent or not so recent university matters.

This book extends through early January 1990, following the announcement of Dr. David P. Roselle's resignation as ninth president of the university and the appointment of Charles T. Wethington, Jr., as interim president. Noting the uncertainty of the moment, Lexington Campus Chancellor Robert Hemenway observed that "We have lost a good president, but we are still a good university. . . . At a difficult time like this, the institution sustains us, gives us faith in ourselves." Indeed, the nature of a university demands accommodation to new knowledge, new people, and outside events. As the University of Kentucky enters its 126th year, it has the means and the spirit of change that will enable it to thrive and to fulfill its mission.

Chapter 1

The Agricultural and Mechanical College
1 8 6 5 - 1 8 7 8

John Bryant Bowman, regent of
Kentucky University (1865-78), had
a majestic vision of higher
education in Kentucky. As the
university and its A&M College
were becoming established in
Lexington, he wrote: "We therefore
want a University with all the
Colleges attached, giving education
of the highest order to all classes.
We want ample grounds and
buildings and libraries, and
apparatus, and museums, and
endowments, and prize-funds, and
professors of great heads and hearts,
men of faith and energy. Indeed we
want everything which will make
this institution eventually equal to
any on this continent. Why should
we not have them? I think we can."
Today the University of Kentucky
stands as a monument to Bowman's
vision.

PREVIOUS PAGE: The former
Tilford home on the Woodlands
farm became the A&M College's
first classroom building. Its upper
floor served as an assembly hall.

The University of Kentucky began humbly as the Agricultural and Mechanical College of the newly formed Kentucky University, a denominational institution that was heir to the diminished glories of Transylvania University.

The A&M College had a special status within Kentucky University. Created by a legislative act of February 22, 1865, it enabled the state of Kentucky to benefit from the federal Morrill Act of 1862, whereby states were entitled to grants of public lands or the equivalent in "land scrip" —330,000 acres in Kentucky's case. The sale of either would provide an endowment fund for the operation of schools, which became known as land grant colleges. Their specified purpose was to offer "such branches of learning as are related to agriculture and the mechanic arts," in addition to "other scientific and classical studies"; military training was also mandated.

Though organized under the umbrella of a private institution, A&M was the state of Kentucky's land grant college. A second legislative act, of February 28, 1865, merged Transylvania University with Kentucky University, and the name "Transylvania" University ceased to exist officially for forty-three years.

The driving genius behind these innovative efforts to revitalize higher education in Kentucky after the Civil War was Harrodsburg farmer and aspiring educator John B. Bowman. Recognizing his vital role in the enactment of the enabling legislation, the Board of Curators of Kentucky University named him regent and treasurer. His was the chief responsibility for getting the university, and particularly its A&M College, under way.

The state law creating the college stipulated that unless within a prescribed time the university raised $100,000 to buy land and provide buildings for the college, the act would not take effect. This challenge inspired Bowman, a persuader who exuded confidence in his vision of a great university in Kentucky. Lexingtonians had been generous to Transylvania in earlier times, and Bowman correctly counted on them to be generous once again. In a matter of months he gathered contributions totaling $125,000, mostly from residents of Lexington and the rest of Fayette County. Sixty-five persons gave $1,000 each—an unusually large gift for the times.

Bowman used the funds to purchase two estates on the southeast edge of Lexington. Woodlands, the smaller, fronting on Richmond Road, was closer to the city and adjoined Ashland, Henry Clay's home farm, at what is now Ashland Avenue. Together, the farms consisted of 433 acres and cost $143,000. The properties were conveyed "for the real estate and building fund of the University," the wording reflecting Bowman's dream of a time when all of Kentucky University might move across the city to the land along Richmond Road.

The A&M College opened on October 1, 1866, with an enrollment of 190 students. It could count on an income of $9,900 a year from the invested proceeds of the scrip sale, plus annual fees of $10 per student—a meager enough budget, but some other institutions of higher learning began no more prosperously. The college also anticipated the sale of farm produce—and crops were indeed bountiful in the first few years—as

While Regent Bowman exercised general supervision of Kentucky University, each of the colleges was headed by a presiding officer—in effect a dean, though the term "president" was commonly used. The first two presidents in the A&M College were John Augustus Williams (left) and Joseph Desha Pickett (right). Each served only three semesters; Pickett was succeeded by James K. Patterson, the first official president. Williams and Pickett are not included in UK's official roster, nor is Bowman.

well as the products of its engineering shops.

The fourteen-room home already standing on Woodlands became the only classroom building, and the second-floor ballroom served as the assembly room. A drill ground for the cadets was marked out between the building and East High Street, the southwest boundary of Woodlands. Regent Bowman, who accepted no salary, occupied the former Clay family home at Ashland. Smaller structures scattered about both farms were pressed into service as dormitories and shops.

Then came an unexpected windfall. A stranger, G.W.N. Yost of Pennsylvania, appeared on campus, seeking—and receiving—help in testing his newly invented mowing machine. In appreciation of the college's services, he gave $25,000 for a building to house the mechanical branch of the school; it was completed by the end of 1868. This unsolicited and very generous gift was one of the most remarkable ever given to the University of Kentucky.

Among the early faculty, some stayed on to make long careers at the institution. The most distinguished was Dr. Robert Peter. He had taught chemistry at Transylvania for some thirty years and would remain at the A&M College for nearly thirty more. Two of his early colleagues, James G. White in mathematics and James K. Patterson in history and moral philosophy, were active into the second decade of the next century. In August 1869, Patterson became the third president of the A&M college; he retired in 1910 after the longest presidential tenure in the university's history.

As he assumed the presidency, Patterson had reason for confidence in the future of the school, despite its inadequacies. The faculty was stable, the student body had increased by 50 percent, and in the preceding term the college had graduated

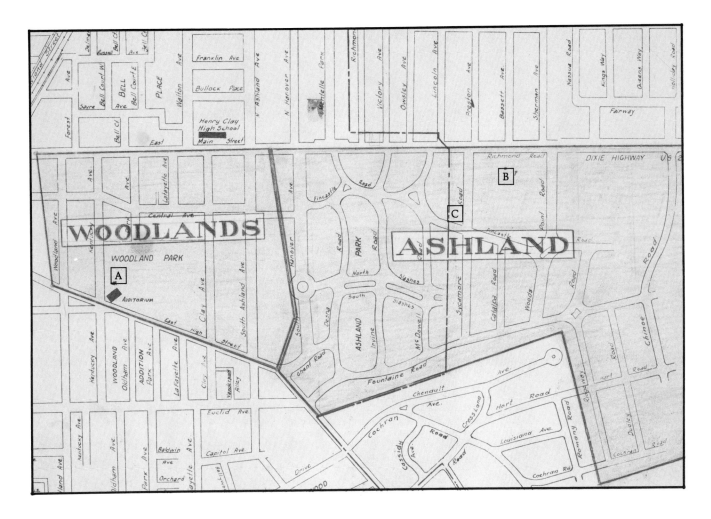

This section of a 1943 street map of Lexington shows the boundaries of the Ashland and Woodlands farms, which lay outside the city limits when the A&M College of Kentucky University was in operation there. The locations of three college buildings—the Tilford home at Woodlands (marked A), the Henry Clay home at Ashland (B), and the Ashland Mechanical Building (C)—are also indicated. In his report to the curators in 1866, Regent Bowman mentioned a possible transfer of the entire university to the Ashland-Woodlands location. Twelve years later the college was separated from the university and in 1882 moved across town to a new campus on South Limestone Street. Eventually, Kentucky University sold the land, which—except for the twenty-acre square surrounding the Henry Clay home—became a residential suburb.

ABOVE: In 1868, G.W.N. Yost's gift of $25,000 was used to construct the Ashland Mechanical Building about 100 yards southwest of the Clay mansion. Lexingtonians liked to visit it on Sunday afternoons, as the picture shows. The building, 60 by 145 feet, housed a mechanical engineering laboratory as well as an implement factory, judging from one extant list of wagons, plows, mowers, and other equipment built there by students. After the college moved away, the building was used as a stable and carriage house until it was demolished in the early 1900s.

OPPOSITE: During its first years the A&M College operated on an annual income of about $13,000. Its main expense was the salaries of faculty and staff, who numbered fourteen in 1880. The janitor received $10 a month and the president (as shown by this voucher) was paid $1,500 a year. After 1880, as a state college, the school began to receive about $20,000 a year from the new half-cent state property tax.

its first student, William B. Munson. It was too early to know that of the young men who enrolled during the early years few would stay the course. By 1878, when the college was separated by legislative fiat from Kentucky University, it had graduated only 14 of the 2,200 who had enrolled during that period.

The terrifying rate of attrition suggests that many illusions were shattered by a brief exposure to life at A&M. The agricultural and mechanical sciences lagged because neither field was built upon firm theoretical and experimental foundations; teaching on the farms and in the shops was merely experiential. The college, and others like it, had not yet become a center for scientific teaching in the areas that gave it its name. Moreover, the Spartan existence required of students may have been more severe than some were willing to endure. Others may have dropped out because the expenses—about $200 a year, including the cost of a uniform— proved too much. Many became distressed when denominational warfare in the 1870s threatened to tear apart both the college and its parent university.

Though it is hard to imagine that 200 or 300 high-spirited young men did not find opportunities for unrecorded highjinks, the demands upon the students left them little time for fun and games. Between reveille and taps in the semimilitary regimen mandated by the Morrill Act, they attended classes, studied the prescribed texts, drilled, and worked in the college's fields and shops. Beyond two hours daily of required manual labor, students could do compensated labor at a rate of ten cents per hour. Throughout the week, those taking classwork on the university's Third Street campus had to hurry back and forth across town; Sundays were taken up with religious observances in the city churches. There were no facilities for sports and recreation. The only sanctioned extracurricular student activity was debate and oratory, organized in 1872 in the Union Literary Society. This early began the university's prominence in forensics, its oldest form of intercollegiate competition and its oldest winning tradition.

But A&M's worst troubles were not of its own making. Sectarian controversy in the Main Street

KENTUCKY UNIVERSITY

No. _____ LEXINGTON.

Lexington, _Sept 20"_ 187_1_.

The bearer has satisfied the requirements for admission to the _A + M_ COLLEGE, and to the several Schools thereof, as far as the following indorsement extends:

Credentials, ... _J. B. Bowman_ Regent.
Consultation, ... _Jos K. Patterson_ Presiding Officer.
English Literature, ... _E. E. Enoch_ Professor.
Mathematics, ... _D. G. Grant_ Professor.
History, ... _Geb Griggs_ _L. E. Smith_ Professor.
Civil and Political Economy, ... Professor.
Chemistry, ... Professor.
Natural Philosophy, ... Professor.
Natural History, ... Professor.
Mental and Moral Philosophy, ... Professor.
Latin Language, ... Professor.
Greek Language, ... Professor.
Hebrew Language, ... Professor.
Modern Languages, ... Professor.
Civil Engineering and Drawing, ... Professor.
Military Science, ... Professor.
Sacred History, ... Professor.
Homiletics and Hermeneutics, ... Professor.
Sacred Literature and Christian Doctrine, ... Professor.
Common and Statute Law, ... Professor.
Constitutional & International Law, ... Professor.
Evidence, Pleading, Practice, ... Professor.
Penmanship, Book-keeping, Commercial Law and Ethics, ... Professor.
Practical Agriculture, ... Superintendent.
Practical Horticulture, ... Superintendent.
Mechanic Arts, ... Superintendent.
Academy, ... Principal.
Payment of Fees, ... _J. B. Bowman_ Treasurer.
Name of Bearer, _Willie Griffing Simpson_
Post Office, _Lexington Ky_
Parent or Guardian, _Mrs Mary R. Simpson_

This paper, when duly endorsed, must be presented, without delay, to the Secretary of the proper Faculty, who is required to matriculate the candidate.

Observer and Reporter print.

ABOVE LEFT: William B. Munson (B.S. 1869) was the first graduate of the A&M College. His brother, Thomas V. Munson (B.S. 1870), was the second. Academic progress was measured at that time not by the accumulation of credit hours but by completion of prescribed studies in the college's several "schools" (departments). The brothers came from Astoria, Illinois, and after graduation made considerable fortunes in northern Texas — William as a railroad builder and financier, Thomas as a nurseryman whose research in practical horticulture won him international recognition.

TOP RIGHT: All the colleges of Kentucky University used the same admission form. This one—for Willie G. Simpson of Lexington— shows that he had satisfied the professors who signed it as to his readiness to study English literature, mathematics, history, and geography at the college level.

Christian Church spread to Kentucky University, and the A&M College could not evade its noxious effects, even though its faculty tried to stay out of the quarrels. Enrollment fell to an all-time low of seventy-eight in 1877-78.

The doctrinal dispute divided the Board of Curators of Kentucky University, two-thirds of whose members had to be members of the Disciples of Christ denomination, the university's parent organization. But when Bowman, who had already been expelled from the Main Street church, offered in 1873 to resign the regency, the majority of the board gave him a vote of confidence. The dissidents prolonged the controversy, and gradually the balance of power on the board shifted. In 1877 the curators abolished the office of regent and subsequently declared Bowman's seat on the board vacant. Removed from Ashland and the university, he took no further part in higher education in Kentucky.

Less out of concern for the university than for the college, with its federal land grant, the legislature sent an investigating committee, which reported widespread sentiment for the separation of the college from the sectarian university. An act of March 13, 1878, cut the umbilical cord, and a commission was named to make temporary arrangements for what was now a state college. The most urgent need was to determine its future site.

Pending a decision for relocation, whether in Lexington or in another city, the college carried on under President Patterson, renting from Kentucky University the land it already occupied.

Dr. Robert Peter holding his son Alfred, ca. 1858. Alfred graduated from State College in 1880, before the move from Woodlands, then became a chemist with the college's Agricultural Experiment Station, where he remained until his retirement in 1927. He died in 1953 at age 96. Father and son together were a part of higher education in Lexington for 120 years through connections with Transylvania University, Kentucky University, Kentucky State College, State University, and the University of Kentucky.

This picture, taken at Woodlands in the 1870s, is the earliest showing Pickett's successor, James K. Patterson, with his faculty grouped around him. Those seated are, left to right: Dr. Robert Peter, professor of chemistry and physics and the most distinguished scholar of the group; President Patterson; an unidentified man; and John Shackelford, professor of English, pastor of the Second Christian Church (which split from the Main Street church during a sectarian dispute), and vice president of State College at the time of his retirement in 1899. Those standing are, left to right: the commandant of cadets, unidentified (serving also as professors of civil engineering, commandants came and went frequently in this period); Francois M. Helveti, who taught modern languages; A.R. Crandall, professor of natural history, formerly with the Kentucky Geological Survey; and James G. White, a beloved professor of mathematics and astronomy and a force for stability until his death in 1913.

Chapter 2

State College
1 8 7 8 - 1 9 0 8

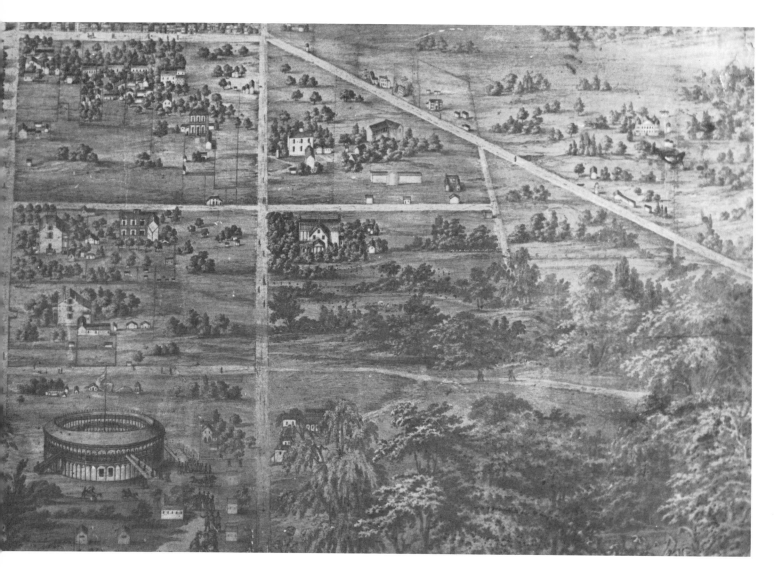

This 1857 pictorial map of Lexington south of High Street (top) and east of Limestone Street (left) shows the area closely connected with State College when it moved in 1882 from the Woodlands-Ashland campus (upper right sector) to the new campus (lower left sector) bounded by Limestone, Winslow Street (now Euclid Avenue), and Rose Street. The fairgrounds amphitheatre (foreground, left) burned down in the meantime.

After its separation from Kentucky University, the A&M College continued at the Ashland-Woodlands site, waiting for the legislature to determine its future. It functioned much as before, the cheering difference being that during the first year of independence, enrollment increased by 50 percent, and observers thought they could detect a lift of morale and spirits among the students and faculty.

In response to the legislative commission's request for offers, only Lexington and Bowling Green tendered serious bids for the college. Lexington took nothing for granted even though the school had been there for thirteen years. President Patterson appeared before the City Council and the Fayette County Court, speaking of the prospects for the college, its importance to Lexington, and the need for community support. The council offered for a campus the fifty-two acre city park and old fairgrounds on South Limestone Street, just beyond the built-up area of town. When Bowling Green bid higher, Lexington raised the ante in two stages to a pledge of $30,000 for buildings, and the Fayette County Court added a pledge of $20,000.

Meeting in Louisville on August 14, 1879, the site commission of the legislature decided to recommend Lexington. The Lexington *Daily Press* editorialized rhapsodically that the council and the court had honorably represented the wishes and interests of Lexington, and "future generations where the history of their present action is read, will have cause to 'rise up and call them blessed.' "

The legislature then performed an unusual act. After approving the site and authorizing Lexington and Fayette County to issue bonds to fulfill their pledges, it gave the college a vote of confidence by enacting for its benefit a permanent tax of half a cent per $100 valuation of taxable property, to be levied annually. Expected in the beginning to produce about $20,000 a year, the tax would become more productive as the state grew. In the year 1881 the college had an income—from this tax, from its land grant endowment, and, for that year only, from the city and county contributions—of about $86,000. The buildings that rose on the new campus stood as reminders of this burst of generosity, though of the first four erected, only the Main Building—the present Administration Building—remains.

The state-appointed Board of Trustees promptly started the construction program. It projected a president's home on campus, a men's dormitory, and a general-purpose classroom-faculty building where the administration—the president and his secretary—would preside. A central plant would provide steam heat. Costly delays slowed the work, however, and building funds were exhausted by mid-1881. The banks refused to lend money, dubious about the fate of the property tax in the next legislature; the vote on the tax had been close in each house, and opposition to it was already being organized. Not until Patterson offered his own funds as collateral could a loan be obtained sufficient to complete construction.

Dedication ceremonies took place on February 15, 1882. Only two days earlier, the dignified faculty and exuberant students had marched down Main Street and out Limestone with bag and baggage to their luxurious new quarters. For the first time the faculty would have offices—that is, each professor would have a desk in an assigned classroom—and the students would enjoy state-of-the-art dormitory quarters. Meanwhile, Lexington filled with dignitaries, who could stroll from the Phoenix Hotel to inspect the campus. Heralding the college's new beginning, the sun shone brightly on dedication day. In the chapel of Main Building, Henry Watterson of the Louisville *Courier-Journal* delivered the address, commending efforts thus far made and expressing hope for the future. He rebuked the legislators, however, calling the half-cent tax a "pittance" inadequate to permit the college to fulfill its expectation of greatness.

The dedication was a personal triumph for Patterson. He had won a great victory just two weeks earlier over foes of the college, who had taken their campaign against the tax to the legislature. Before a joint session of the two houses on January 30, 1882, Patterson argued for the constitutionality of the tax. He spoke, he said, as a historian, not as a lawyer, as he passionately defend-

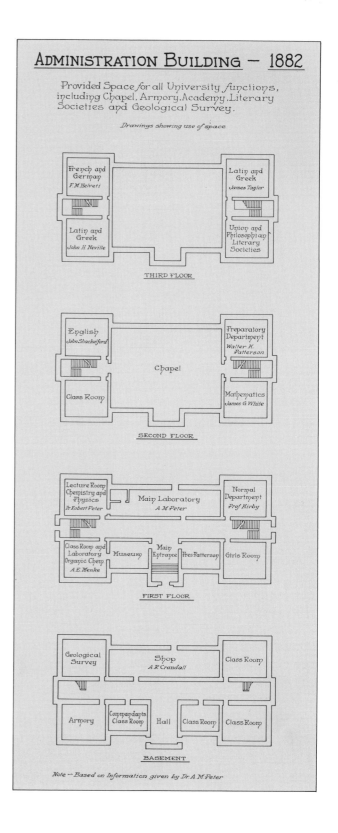

ADMINISTRATION BUILDING — 1882

Provided Space for all University functions, including Chapel, Armory, Academy, Literary Societies and Geological Survey.

Drawings showing use of space

Note — Based on Information given by Dr A.M. Peter

OPPOSITE: This chart, drawn in 1945 on the basis of information supplied by Alfred M. Peter, who had been on campus in 1882, shows the original allocations in Main Building. In 1882 and for some years afterward, it was indeed the main building: all academic functions took place there, and professors' classrooms doubled as their offices. Today the stairways and two lower hallways remain as in this chart. Otherwise the interior is the result of many rearrangements.

ABOVE: The college's new buildings stand stark against the wintry sky. Behind Main Building (now the Administration Building) is the chimney of the heating plant. In the distance to the left is the president's home. The commandant's home (a house already on the property) peeks out to the right of the dormitory.

The president's home stood on the site now occupied by the east end of the White Hall classroom building. The Pattersons were its only residents. After his death, the Faculty Club and, for a few years, offices occupied it until its demolition in the mid-1960s.

LEFT: President Patterson's office was in the space now occupied by the inner office of the chancellor of the Lexington campus. The crutch visible here and evident in most pictures of Patterson was necessary because of an injury incurred during his early childhood in Scotland.

ed the very existence of the college. For two and a half hours he overwhelmed the legislators with his knowledge, reasoning powers, and eloquence in the greatest speech ever delivered by a president of the University of Kentucky. He concluded with an exhortation: "Let Kentucky rouse from her slumber, shake off her lethargy, and in the provision she makes for the education of her sons dare to be free."

The tax also survived subsequent attempts to destroy the principle that the legislature could appropriate money for higher education. The question thereafter was not whether the legislature had the power to appropriate but how much it would provide.

After victory in the legislature and occupation of the three new buildings, Patterson could look about the campus proudly and observe the largest student body yet, 318, and a faculty grown to 17. The curriculum was richer accordingly. Adjunct to State College (as it soon came to be called) was a Normal School for the training of teachers and an Academy for students preparing to attend college. The faculty had received salary increases the year before: senior professors now earned $1,500 a year; Patterson received $2,000 and perquisites, including pasturage for his cows down the slope from the new president's home into the area along Winslow Street that would soon become athletic fields.

Because a large proportion of the teachers in the state's common schools were women, their enrollment in the Normal School had been argued and agreed to almost as soon as the school opened on the old Woodlands campus just before the move. Inevitably, women soon came to be accepted in regular degree programs at State Col-

ABOVE: In 1901, horticulture was located in the Natural Science Building (now Miller Hall); the top floor housed the horticulture museum.

RIGHT: Two faculty stalwarts on the campus were Paul Anderson and Joseph Kastle. Anderson lived on until 1935, serving as dean of the unified College of Engineering after 1921. A short man, he may have chosen his footing for this picture. Joseph Kastle was an alumnus of State College who earned a doctorate in chemistry at Johns Hopkins, taught at State College, Hopkins, and the University of Virginia, and returned to State University in 1911. He succeeded Melville Scovell as dean of the College of Agriculture and director of the Experiment Station in 1912. He died in 1916.

lege, all without a stir. In 1884, Leonora Hoeing of Lexington received the first Normal School diploma awarded to a woman, and four years later Belle Clement Gunn of Lexington was awarded the first State College degree earned by a woman. The newspapers wrote ecstatically of the accomplishments of these "Scholastic Maidens." In this respect State College was a leader in the South, just as in 1949, when blacks gained admission to the University of Kentucky's graduate and professional schools without demonstrations or resistance.

From the time it moved to South Limestone Street, State College experienced slow growth, gradual curriculum enrichment, and quiet academic improvement. The two most notable forward steps in the first decade were the establishment of the Agricultural Experiment Station and a department of mechanical engineering under the dynamic young Paul Anderson. Other advances that occurred, though not spectacular, endured because as they came about they were built firmly into the fabric of the school.

To illustrate: In 1882 the college's regular income was about $30,000, not counting fees; by 1908, when the legislature renamed the college State University, its income was $116,000. While income was increasing fourfold, enrollment increased only 50 percent, to 477 in 1908. Faculty and staff numbered eighty-two in the latter year, a remarkable growth in relation to income and enrollment increases. In its first commencement on the new campus the college awarded only six degrees; in its last year as State College it granted 101 degrees, mostly undergraduate. Other figures speak to the institution's original mission as an agricultural and mechanical school: in 1908 the

Once the faculty was quartered with him in Main Building, Patterson (center front with his crutch) could easily summon them for picturetaking, as here in 1886. Those of more than temporary association with State College are as follows: The two to Patterson's left are James G. White, mathematics, and, in the top hat, John Shackelford, English. On the third step to the left are Robert Peter, chemistry, and his son Alfred, by then with the Experiment Station. Topmost at upper right is Maurice Kirby of the Normal Department; below him and to his right, with the white beard, is Francois M. Helveti, French and German; and to his left, behind Shackelford, is Walter K. Patterson, the president's brother and principal of the Academy. Topmost at left is Albert A. Menke, agriculture; to his left, A.R. Crandall, natural history; and the daring one without a hat, John H. Neville, classics.

In the open window is Patterson's eighteen-year-old son, William Andrew. After graduating from State College he taught English as an assistant to Shackelford, 1891-95. In ill health during these years, he died during the 1895 commencement season.

TOP: *The evolution of a building: The original Experiment Station, the first building to go up after the original three, was completed in 1889 at a cost of $20,000. In 1891 it was destroyed by fire and rebuilt immediately on the same plans. It was later home to chemistry (1905), law (1925), hygiene, public health, and an infirmary (1939). Since 1962, as Gillis Hall, it has housed the registrar's and admissions office.*

BOTTOM: *The second building added to the original three, the "new dormitory" (later Neville Hall) was built in 1890 just behind the Experiment Station.*

engineering departments produced fifty-two of the degree recipients—but only two degrees were in agriculture. Although the statistics tell of a generally improved institution and greater opportunities for students, State College was not keeping up with its neighbors in surrounding states. The teaching area in agriculture was recognized as laggard, but it was on the eve of a transfusion of energy.

To the passerby on the South Limestone trolley or a member of the public strolling about the campus of a Sunday afternoon in 1908, the physical growth of the college was evident. The original buildings were surrounded along a northeast-south arc by a campus and Experiment Station farm of 291 acres. After the city's initial gift of 52 acres, the college had purchased parcels of adjoining land as they became available. Newer structures clustered around the superintending presence of Main Building, except for the 1905 Experiment Station Building at the corner of Washington Avenue and South Limestone Street, closer to the farm.

All the post-1882 buildings were erected with money saved out of income plus legislative appropriations and a gift from Patterson's friend Andrew Carnegie. They included those now known as Barker Hall, Frazee Hall, Gillis Hall, Miller Hall, the Mathews Building, Patterson Hall—all still in use—as well as several that have been demolished: the lovely little Carnegie Library, President Patterson's home, Neville Hall (built as a dormitory), and White Hall, the original dormitory. Both dorms had been converted to classroom and other uses. In 1908, the view from the city dump on the west side of Limestone Street looking up toward Main Build-

ABOVE: Patterson Hall, the first women's dormitory and the only one built entirely at state expense, was included in the special $60,000 building appropriation of 1900 that also provided for the building of Alumni (Barker) Hall. The last word in dormitory construction, it was located across Winslow Street (Euclid Avenue) as the first excursion beyond the original campus. It became the nucleus of a complex of women's dorms at the corner of Euclid Avenue and Limestone Street.

LEFT: The gymnasium in Alumni (Barker) Hall was used by both men and women for physical education and basketball until 1924, when the women were given exclusive domain. Here, a group of coeds works out in hope of "banishing awkwardness."

The Limestone Street campus bordered on the Mulligan property line running parallel to Rose Street from Winslow Street to Washington Avenue. At the bottom of the hill on which the new campus buildings stood flowed a narrow stream fed by Mulligan Spring. Halfway to Limestone St. it received overflow from Maxwell Spring and spread out into a marsh. Eventually the water passed under the street and found its way into Town Branch. Mulligan Spring, shown here, was a pleasant spot for students to gather.

ing and the old dorm no longer presented the stark appearance it had in 1882; it had been softened by landscaping, and trees grown larger over the past twenty-five years.

Still, however impressed they may have been by the appearance of the campus, outsiders and newspapers were often critical of its academic life. The Academy drained effort and money from a college struggling to pass for an institution of higher learning. The presence of the Academy as well as the Normal School in college buildings tended to lower the tone of the campus. Except for the Experiment Station staff and the members of the chemistry department, which worked with

it, few among the faculty were serious research scholars. Heavy teaching loads, other assigned duties, and lack of facilities impeded research among instructors of whom in 1908 only two held doctoral degrees. Teaching was almost entirely the dissemination of textbook information. Serious deficiencies, notably in agriculture, were the subject of considerable criticism. In 1907 the trustees provided funds for a new agriculture building (in addition, that is, to the Experiment Station, which had always had its own building and whose mission was from the beginning agricultural research) and for additional faculty trained in the agricultural sciences.

With the absence of adequate high schools
in the 19th century, many colleges
maintained preparatory schools to ready
young people for college. President
Patterson's younger brother, Walter K.
Patterson (right), was principal of the State
College Academy (above) from its
establishment in 1880 until it closed in
1911.

The facts of Walter's career have been
mixed with malicious campus gossip, yet he
lobbied for tax-supported higher education in
the Constitutional Convention of 1890-91
and in the 1900 General Assembly session,
which appropriated $60,000 for the women's
dormitory and for Alumni Hall. He was also
superintendent of construction for the dorm
and even served for a short time as its assistant "matron," earning the nickname "She
Pat."

But elsewhere on campus there were distinct and significant achievements. As new faculty were added, degree majors such as English, ancient languages, and history replaced the old classics curriculum; specialization was setting in. In the 1890s anatomy and physiology became a department under Joseph W. Pryor, M.D., and Merry Lewis Pence found his permanent place as head of the new department of physics. In response to outside urging, mining engineering became a department in 1901. With the completion of Barker Hall (first known as Alumni Hall) in 1902, a new gymnasium could accommodate departments of physical education for women and men and basketball for both. Four years later the trustees established a department of domestic economy (home economics).

If an enriched curriculum expanded students' academic lives, their campus and social lives were still severely restricted by a multitude of regulations decreed by trustees and faculty. One bizarre rule prohibited reading material other than textbooks in students' quarters "without permission from the President." Only a saint could have avoided infraction of one or another of the nearly 200 published rules. Violations could bring such punishments as demerits or "confinement to quarters"—terminology bespeaking the continuing status of male students as cadets living in a quasi-military regimen and required to take four years (reduced to three in 1907) of military science.

Yet gradually campus life was becoming more relaxed, and opportunities for sports, recreation, and social events were increasing. Students showed some initiative about asking for changes, and the authorities more consideration in grant-

President Patterson enjoys a quiet moment on his porch.

ing them. As early as 1893 the faculty approved by a vote of 14 to 3 a student petition for fraternities on campus, and chapters of Kappa Alpha and Sigma Chi were founded before the year ended. Fourteen years later a chapter of Alpha Xi Delta sorority appeared. In 1901 the trustees acceded to the petition of a student committee to hold dances in the gym or the armory of Barker Hall, then nearing completion. Barker Hall served many purposes and contributed to an amelioration of student life.

Some campus activities were held in high regard. Four literary societies, two each for men and women, conducted debate and oratory sessions in their assigned rooms in Barker Hall and Main Building. Campus championship and intercollegiate contests at the new Broadway Opera House in town or in the college chapel, with the competitors in formal attire, produced winners who became campus notables. Clark Tandy, state intercollegiate oratory champion in 1901 and 1903, went to Oxford as one of the first American contingent of Rhodes Scholars.

The cadet band originally played mainly for military reviews, but the coming of football in 1892 provided a new outlet for band perfor-

The first woman to receive a degree from State College, which became coeducational after 1880, was Belle Clement Gunn of Lexington (B.S. 1888). She was one of six students awarded earned degrees that year. The Lexington "Daily Press" described this "strikingly handsome young lady" as "a bright flower in the soberly hued meadow" of male graduates.

ABOVE: Yearbooks and anecdotes indicate that State College students were less oppressed than the stern campus rules suggest. Their humor was often just short of irreverent. This 1894 yearbook sketch was hardly a prototype of the sweetheart of Sigma Chi, a fraternity new on campus the year before.

OPPOSITE: Grouped on the steps of the recently built Experiment Station building (now Gillis Hall), these modishly dressed young ladies were the female enrollees of State College in 1892, many undoubtedly in the Normal School.

RIGHT: Many male State College students lived in dormitories from the time the college moved to the new campus. But after a 1917 investigating committee reported that both "old" and "new" men's dorms ought to be condemned as public nuisances, the buildings were converted to classroom and office space and new dorms were planned.

The rivalry between the two Lexington schools, Kentucky State College and Kentucky University, was as keen on the debate platform as in any other arena. At State College, the Union Literary Society (1872) and the Patterson Literary Society (1887) enjoyed great prestige, sponsoring campus forensic contests and sending representatives to intercollegiate competitions. Clark Howell Tandy (B.A. 1903, left), a Patterson member, was the school's best-known public speaker, winning the state intercollegiate oratorical championship in 1901 and 1903. Tandy also became his alma mater's first Rhodes Scholar.

BELOW: State College students were favored in the number of good picnic spots available to them. High Bridge was a favorite. Sports clothes were unknown, and even for such violent recreations as flag rushes the warriors dressed in shirts and trousers.

mances. Students sometimes organized informal groups that might last as long as an academic generation—the Mandolin Club was one such—or put on plays in the chapel, attracting enthusiastic audiences.

Occasionally students felt the urge to do something daring or rowdy, and to indulge it they showed remarkable inventiveness, especially on Halloween. President Patterson's horse was no stranger to the chapel stage on the second floor of Main Building and knew what it was like to be painted green. The cannon in front of Main Building now and then might be seen tipped on its side of a morning, and a party of visiting dignitaries once emerged from the building to find their carriage resting on its axles. City policemen carried out missions to State College grudgingly, apprehensive about their reception,

though it was only a mild harassment to have water poured on their heads if they passed within range of upper-story windows. And entering freshmen probably wondered what devilish new forms of hazing awaited them.

I n 1892, with the faculty showing a tolerant interest and the administration—Patterson—a look-the-other-way indifference, the students, following two years of unorganized efforts, determined to make something of the game of football. They scheduled matches with neighboring colleges and persuaded a new, young geology professor, Arthur Miller, to coach the team on the presumption that because he had attended Princeton, he knew something about the game.

The formation of the State College Broom Brigade in 1888 may have been inspired by Mark Twain's description, in "Life on the Mississippi" (1883), of broom brigades he saw in the South and West. They performed intricate drills for the public. The State College brigade was a precursor of cadet sponsors and later ROTC units. Identified by Anne Y. McConnell of the College of Library and Information Science, the 1888 Broom Brigade was composed of (left to right): unidentified; Minnie Moore, later a schoolteacher; Mrs. Ernest Cassity, Minnie's sister; Sally Belle Baker; Mayme Combs; Elmer Allen; Kate Baker; Hattie Warner; Annie J. Baker; and Sallie Hornbrook; and on the steps, Mary Lou Baker, Virgie Hearne, and Joe Hearne.

This artillery drill on the hillside
below the old dorm must have been
well advertised. The "reviewing
stand" in the background is the
gymnasium floor of Alumni Hall,
then under construction.

RIGHT: What a difference a year
makes! This young man entered
State College but will graduate from
State University.

President Patterson displayed little interest in the arts, and the State College program included no music. But the cadet band went naturally with the cadet corps. Here Herman Trost, who taught music at Hamilton College, a Lexington girls' school, stands (left, second row) with his 1893 State College band.

Midway into their season they procured a new coach who did in fact know something about the game, having played at Purdue. John A. Thompson actually played in a game for State College that season; no rule prohibited the coach from doing so. The team won two games, lost four, and tied one.

Before the next season the Central Kentucky colleges formed the Kentucky Intercollegiate Athletic Association (KIAA) for the purpose, mainly, of formulating rules. In 1893 something portentous occurred: Coach Thompson led his team to Knoxville where State beat Tennessee 56-0, the most lopsided score in the history of the rivalry between the schools. That game was not only the beginning of the Kentucky-Tennes-

see competition but, if a point is stretched, the first small step in the direction of a southward orientation in Kentucky athletics.

The magic of football as a spectator sport exerted itself almost at once. Main Street businessmen and some faculty members, most of them strangers to the game, formed a stock company. From the proceeds of stock sales, with labor donated by engineering students, and with Patterson's cows evicted, the grounds were improved and enclosed by a fence, and wooden stands were erected on both sides of the field. The college authorities assigned supervision of football, baseball, and track to a faculty committee of three, though the active management of the teams devolved upon three student managers,

In 1898, the seventh season of organized football at State College, the players earned a place in the university's record book as its only undefeated—indeed, unscored-upon—team. Sportswriters still speak with awe of the "Immortals" who in seven games racked up a total score of 181-0 against Kentucky University, Georgetown, Louisville Athletic Club, Centre, Newcastle A.C., and two military teams recruited from units in training in Lexington during the Spanish-American War. The team's coach, W.R. Bass, once substituted for an ailing player. The crowd at one game numbered four hundred— no larger than that at the Patterson Literary Society's declamatory contest the night before.

one for each sport, elected by students who became members of the athletic association by buying season tickets. When basketball was added in 1903, a fourth manager joined the others in performing a variety of functions—including the scheduling of games—that would later be done by athletic directors and ticket and equipment managers. The job of student manager was not an empty honor; each one was fully entitled to the status of campus personality, and together they rated a separate page in the yearbook.

As in other schools, the competitiveness of athletics brought its problems. On October 27, 1893, Professor James P. Nelson, professor of civil engineering, reported to the faculty a decision of the athletic committee that "only bona-fide State College students" could be members of teams.

The ruling was made necessary by "ringers," who were drifting around among colleges playing under assumed names. In 1901 the *Kentucky Magazine* claimed: "The State College has stood and will stand for purity in athletics. 'Ringers' are not recognized in this school. Each member of the team is a student and a gentleman."

From 1892 through 1907 State College football teams had nine winning and seven losing seasons. They played Indiana, Purdue, Ohio State, Virginia, Vanderbilt, and West Virginia in addition to their Bluegrass rivals in the KIAA. State's first game against Centre in 1893 was its only loss that season, beginning a rivalry that continued until 1929. In 1908 football was still the major sport and could early be seen as a money maker. Though the institution had

This action shot shows why football aroused so much spectator interest. Around 1900, spectators at State College football games, if they did not stand along the sidelines, sat in small wooden stands erected by engineering students. Attendance at games became fashionable, partly because they were dress-up occasions. The two ladies with big white mums were helping to establish a college football tradition that died only recently.

The women's basketball team of 1902-3 was the first of either sex at State College to play a full intercollegiate schedule. In the front row, left to right, are Miriam Nave, Alice Pence, Nell Norwood, Fanny Redd, and an unidentified player. In the second row, far left, is Amanda Maull; the last two on the right are Helen Jaeger and Willie Spier. Standing in the rear center are Jane Todd Watson (coach) and Jimmie Offutt; a head lower on the far right is Mary E. Clarke.

formed no out-of-state connections that threatened to take it away from the KIAA, signs pointed in that direction, especially after Tennessee and Vanderbilt became fixtures on the schedule.

Basketball lagged behind, arriving later than football on most college campuses. At State there was no place to play until Barker Hall was built, and even then it was not a spectator sport for the simple reason that the gym could not accommodate more than those who could stand around the floor of the balcony, which was also the running track. From 1903 on, the men shared the gym with the women, who had organized a team a year earlier.

Concentrated in the months of January and February, basketball for some twenty years seemed merely an interlude between the end of football season in November and the time for baseball and track. The physical education director, Walter Mustaine, served officially and reluctantly as men's coach for five years while the student manager and team captain actually coached the players. That may explain basketball's poor start. Between 1903 and 1908, for example, State lost three of four games with the Lexington YMCA.

Baseball and track attracted larger crowds, but no records of the spring sports have been compiled for these early years. Students paid more attention to them than the newspapers did; the existence of professional baseball and the revival in 1896 of the Olympic games powerfully stimulated interest.

At State College, as elsewhere, intercollegiate athletic competition quickly became an established part of the college program—earlier than many modern academic units in the arts and sciences. The athletic program was old enough in 1908 to be a tradition, and football was already big stuff. Kentucky sports entered the big time not by gradual growth but by irregularly spaced upward leaps during the next three decades.

In the golden mist of fond memories of old "State," alumni of that early period thought of themselves as special people. As early as 1889, sixty or so living graduates formed an alumni association. By the end of its career in 1908, State College had awarded 738 bachelor's degrees and 108 master's degrees. Patterson encouraged alumni to return to the campus at commencement time. Once assembled, members conducted their association meetings, and old grads gathered at the Phoenix Hotel to reminisce.

The careers of alumni are measures of a college as an institution of higher learning. Since the first woman graduated in 1888, 141 "Scholastic Maidens" had followed her across the commencement platform, though men had earned all of the master's degrees. Engineering degrees—most of them earned after 1900—were nearly 38 percent of the total earned degrees, not surprising in an agricultural and mechanical school in a period when the nation's industries were growing and diversifying and demanding trained engineers. For the next twenty years, engineering students were more prominent in campus affairs than they would be afterwards.

Many graduates desiring professional or advanced degrees had to go on to other institutions because State College did not offer law or medicine or graduate work at the doctoral level. It was primarily an undergraduate institution. Nevertheless, the work it offered was substantial enough to propel many of its alumni into notable careers. Its first two graduates, the Munson brothers from Illinois, set challenging precedents.

For the first half of this century, Richard C. Stoll was intimately associated with State College, State University, and the University of Kentucky. He was appointed to the Board of Trustees three years after graduating in 1895 at age 22 and, except for one three-year interval, served on the board until his death in 1949. Stoll Field was named for him.

Three early alumni became members of the college's faculty: Alfred Peter (1880), Merry Lewis Pence (1881), and the distinguished scientist Joseph Kastle (1884). Also joining the faculty were George Roberts in agronomy (1899) and William Webb in physics (1901). James Hiram Graham (1900) earned distinction as an engineer, especially in World War I, and returned as dean of engineering from 1935 to 1940. Two Lexingtonians, Richard C. Stoll (1895), for whom Stoll Field was named, and Louis Hillenmeyer (1907), became prominent in Lexington as lawyer and judge and as nurseryman respectively, with both serving many years as trustees of their alma mater.

Other graduates made distinguished careers outside Kentucky. For example, J. Irwin Lyle, an early football regular, earned bachelor's and master's degrees in engineering in the late 1890s. He helped found and was president of the Carrier Engineering Corporation, specializing in refrigeration and air conditioning, and brought several other alumni into executive positions in that company. He served as president of the National Alumni Association and as a trustee. James G. Scrugham (1900) went to Nevada, joined the engineering faculty of its university, turned to politics in 1923, and was elected successively as governor, U.S. congressman, and senator. Frank Daugherty (1901) accepted a position with Scovell Engineering Company in Philadelphia, where he specialized in the design and construction of water, gas, and electrical systems. James W. Carnahan (1896), organizer of Lyons & Carnahan in Chicago, concentrated on publishing textbooks. William C. McCarty (1900) studied medicine at Johns Hopkins and became a pathologist at the Mayo Clinic and the University of Minnesota Medical School.

Three men of prominence who attended State but did not graduate included Henry Stites Barker (1869-71) who left to study law and later became a judge of the Court of Appeals, a trustee of State College, and successor to Patterson as president. A.O. Stanley, who was at State in 1886-88, served in both houses of Congress with the governor-

Five of State College's most distinguished alumni: left to right, J. Irwin Lyle, James G. Scrugham, James W. Carnahan, Crawford H. Ellis, and Thomas Hunt Morgan.

ship (1915-19) sandwiched between, then stayed in Washington as chairman of the American-Canadian International Joint Commission. A student in 1892-93, Crawford H. Ellis had a spectacular career with the United Fruit Company and as an organizer and president of the Pan-American Life Insurance Company of New Orleans.

The most eminent of all Lexingtonians and of all State College alumni was Thomas Hunt Morgan, who between 1886 and 1890 earned bachelor's and master's degrees at State and the Ph.D. at Johns Hopkins. After professorships of zoology at Bryn Mawr, Columbia, and the California Institute of Technology, he received the 1933 Nobel Prize in Medicine for his studies in heredity and genetics.

As early as 1897 President Patterson asked the Board of Trustees whether the size and complexity of the college justified changing its status to university. His reasons were clear. The federal Hatch Act of 1887 had provided for federally subsidized agricultural experiment stations in the states and in effect had blessed the college's establishment of a station two years earlier. A new building was provided at once, and the station's research and testing work soon eclipsed the teaching of the agricultural department. With departments springing up, the college was extending itself beyond the mission suggested by its name.

Aware of these changes, the trustees were ready to think seriously about university status, though they hesitated over Patterson's suggestion for adding law and medicine to the college. The denominational Kentucky University helped to resolve potential confusion by its willingness to resume the venerable name of Transylvania University. As the matter came into public discussion, legislators, the new Eastern and Western Kentucky Normal Schools, and the constituencies of both Lexington institutions showed friendly interest in the idea of a state university in Kentucky—reflecting a change in public attitudes since the controversies of the previous decade.

The law signed on March 16, 1908, went beyond the mere declaration of the new name, "State University, Lexington, Kentucky." It included an enlightened statement dedicating the institution to teaching and "original research," and it stipulated structural changes consonant with the status of a university. Agriculture and mechanical arts (engineering) should have collegiate status. Further, though not using the word "college," the legislation specified the introduction of "courses of instruction" leading to degrees in medicine and law. In another act, this education-minded legislature specified that a department of education should replace the old Normal School and offer instruction of "collegiate rank" leading to the bachelor's degree in education. This act also appropriated $200,000 for capital improvements.

At last Kentucky had a state university.

The chapel platform was large enough in the early days to seat the entire faculty. Students marched in military formation to the daily exercises at 8:30 A.M. Here, President Patterson presides.

The first dormitory ("old dorm") was later renovated for other uses as White Hall, named for James G. White, professor of mathematics and vice-president at the time of his death in 1913.

Merry Pence (above) and Joseph Pryor (in photo at right), a medical doctor who taught anatomy and physiology, collaborated in the construction of this X-ray machine, built in 1896 within months after professional journals published

Wilhelm Roentgen's reports of his researches. It was the only such machine in town, and Pence and Pryor performed X-rays for local doctors, both in the hospital and in Pence's home, searching for needles and bullets and treating cancers.

Pence's work is regarded as the beginning of genuine research in the physics department. Parts of the machine are on display in that department.

BELOW: Edwin S. Good came to State College in 1906 and within a few years accomplished some of the most significant research in the history of UK. The Good Barn near the football stadium is named for him but only barely suggests his immense contributions to livestock industries. In 1911 Good identified the organism that caused infectious abortion in mares and soon developed a serum for immunization, thereby saving the horse industry. He went on to achieve a national reputation for his work in livestock nutrition and diseases.

Clarence W. Mathews came to State College in 1892 as professor of horticulture, the central study in agriculture at that time. Not until 1908 was the College of Agriculture created, with Mathews as its first dean. In 1910 it came together with the Experiment Station under M.A. Scovell as dean and director. Mathews remained as head of the department of horticulture until his death in 1928.

Melville A. Scovell came to State College to head the Agricultural Experiment Station on its establishment in 1885. With federal funds, the station was more affluent than any other unit in the college. Patterson complained that it functioned as a kind of entity unto itself rather than working in close harmony with the department of agriculture. In 1910, two years before his death, Scovell also became dean of the College of Agriculture, an important step toward integrating all agricultural units under one person. But another decade passed before full integration was achieved. The present Experiment Station Building bears Scovell's name.

Posing on the steps of the Natural Science Building in 1907, the last year of State College, is part of its faculty. Does it say anything, even in this small sample, that the two female faculty members were in math and science?

Left to right, the faculty are, row 1: Milford White, Normal School; Alexander St. Clair Mackenzie, English; Clarence W. Mathews, botany; John Henry Neville, classics and college vice-president; President Patterson; James G. White, mathematics; and Major Wilson

Bryant Burtt, commandant of cadets. Row 2 (all on the second step): Merry L. Pence, physics; Franklin E. Tuttle, chemistry; Alfred C. Zembrod, modern languages; and Walter E. Rowe, rural engineering. Row 2 1/2 (a step higher between the second and third rows in the middle): Arthur M. Miller, geology; and Joseph W. Pryor, anatomy and physiology. Row 3: Arthur Fleshman, Normal School; Leon K. Frankel, mechanical engineering; T.T. Jones, classics; John Leslie Purdom,

Academy; Knox Jameson, Academy; A.M. Wilson, mechanical engineering; and Martha White, mathematics.

Top row: Cotton Noe, Normal School; William J. Carrell, civil engineering; J. Morton Davis, mathematics; Alfred Haley Gilbert, botany; Alfred McGregor, Academy; Harry D. Easton, mining engineering; Alfred Newlon Whitlock, Academy; Sue D. McCann, zoology, entomology, botany; and William S. Webb, physics.

ABOVE: Students pose in a lab in the new chemistry building (old Experiment Station), 1907.

RIGHT: A view from the top of Main Building shows the first unit of Kastle Hall in the upper left quadrant. Below it, at left, is Natural Science (1898; later Miller Hall), and at the lower right the "new" dorm of 1890. In the middle are the engineering buildings, the nearest thing to a complex of related buildings until recent times.

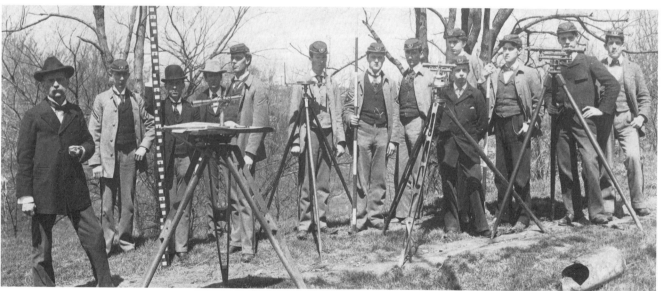

The teaching of the "mechanic" arts was written into the Morrill Act, which established the land grant colleges. The engineering class in the top photo was taught by Louis Nollau (seen at right), whose photography added so much to our early view of the university. The photo of the student surveyors at work is from an earlier era, and little is known about the subjects. Note their cadet-type uniforms.

Alumni (Barker) Hall, occupied in 1902, was perhaps the most useful building the campus ever knew. With classrooms, a gymnasium, and an armory, it greatly enlarged academic, social, and recreational opportunities. Dances were held there, as well as physical education classes and basketball games. In the winter of 1988-89, the tower acquired a bell for the first time.

In 1905, when the Experiment Station with its laboratory work outgrew its old building, it moved to this new one (right). Located at Washington Avenue and Limestone Street, the new building was closer to the farm—which was pushing southward toward open land—and reasonably close to the Agriculture Building. Its classic front was unusual on the UK campus, and with its later wings it impressed by a size uncommon at the university prior to World War II.

RIGHT: John Henry (Jack) Neville (d. 1908), who taught Greek and Latin, was a character at State College. He was seldom seen without his umbrella and generally read a book as he walked along. Belying his appearance, he had a sharp wit—and great hopes for the school as well. In 1896, after a state senator blasted the college for its inadequacy, Neville wrote a reply signed by twenty-seven of his colleagues. He spoke for every generation of UK faculty members: "Our work is hard and our compensation moderate . . . but if we are not interfered with we shall make this college what it has ever been our ambition to make it, the pride not merely of Lexington but of the whole Commonwealth."

BOTTOM: In 1890 the trustees commissioned Merry L. Pence to survey prospects for a lake to be fed by the Mulligan and Maxwell springs. On July 8, 1890, Pence reported that for about $4,500 the college could construct a lake a quarter-mile long, six feet deep at the Limestone end and three at the upper end. The result was a pleasant spot for summer boating and winter skating, but in about twenty years nature and "progress" had turned it into a swamp and restoration was not feasible. The problem was resolved during the early 1920s by grading and channeling during preparation of the grounds for building Alumni Gymnasium and McLean Stadium.

The boardinghouse, a nineteenth-century institution, has virtually disappeared from the American scene. Students who did not live in the dorms often boarded around the area of the campus as late as the 1920s, usually on Rose Street or South Limestone. To judge from appearances, not all the residents were State College students. The boardinghouse brought town and gown together.

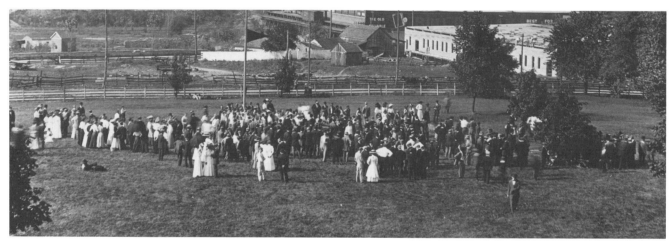

By the turn of the century, with the annual number of degrees in double digits, the June commencement was of great importance in the life of the college and the social life of Lexington. A commencement procession preceded the ceremonies, which took place in a tent in front of Main Building.

"Just before the battle, mother!" The pennant on the pole at center will be the sophomore attackers' goal, with freshmen defending in the 1909 annual flag rush. On American campuses in those days, class competitions in one form or another were big events. The practice lasted into the 1920s.

Chapter 3

State University
1908-1916

PREVIOUS PAGE: This painting by Arthur J. Elder shows the campus of State University in 1911. An inaccurate representation in some respects, it nevertheless reminds us that the university was on the southern edge of the city and emphasizes how the campus buildings huddled together on the hill. Three of those shown here—Carnegie Library, Pence Hall, and Kastle Hall—were the only ones built during State University's time and were planned during the waning days of State College.

ABOVE: Assembled on the steps of the new Education Building (now Frazee Hall) is the first class in the College of Law, which opened in the fall of 1908, the year State College became State University. At right in the front row is Judge William T. Lafferty, who gave up his seat on the Board of Trustees to become dean of the College of Law.

In converting a college into a university, the president and trustees acted promptly on some matters and hesitantly, when at all, on others.

They formed three engineering colleges—civil, mechanical and electrical, and mining—thus evading the delicate personnel decisions that would have been involved in creating a comprehensive engineering college.

The department of agriculture became a college which in 1910 was unified with the Experiment Station, then under Melville Amasa Scovell; he thus became dean of the College of Agriculture as well as director of the station. (When the federal Smith-Lever Act of 1914 provided subsidies for the Agricultural Extension Service, Scovell was dead, and it was several more years before the three parts of the work in agriculture were integrated under one dean.)

In comparison, the creation of a College of Law was easy and inexpensive, there being no conflicting vested interests to reconcile. Judge W.T. Lafferty, already a member of the Board of Trustees, eagerly accepted the deanship and the commission to get the college under way forthwith. It went into operation in the fall of 1908, with the dean and two part-time teachers providing instruction for thirty students.

Medical instruction was a more complex matter. The president and trustees approached it gingerly and, after study, did nothing.

The other legislative mandates presented no difficulties. A College of Arts and Science brought together the several departments that had formerly made up the classics (humanities) and science divisions. Its new dean was Arthur M. Miller of geology, who sixteen years earlier had been temporarily the football coach.

A department of education replaced the Normal School, with authority to certify teachers for the public schools and to recommend to the trustees candidates for new bachelor of education degrees. Until 1923, except for a two-year experiment with a Teachers College between 1909 and 1911, education remained a department in the College of Arts and Science. It was authorized to start a Model School in place of the Academy, but several years elapsed before the University High School was fully in operation.

Comprising, then, the College of Agriculture, the College of Arts and Sciences, three engineering colleges, and (the only new area of study) the College of Law, with the Experiment Station still a separate entity, in 1908 the institution structurally met the criterion of a university com-

Henry Stites Barker, president of State University, 1910-17. A good man and an able judge, he came to the presidency handicapped by his nonacademic background.

posed of colleges. Nomenclature said nothing, however, about the academic strength of the components.

With the State University a reality, President Patterson ended speculation about his retirement. The 1909 commencement celebrated his fortieth year in the presidency, and the next day he announced to the trustees his intention to step down when a successor was appointed.

Patterson did not resign formally until the end of the year; in the meantime a search committee of the board, the first in the institution's history, was gravitating toward a well-known Kentuckian. But not until June 1, 1910, did Judge Henry Stites Barker appear before the board to read his letter of acceptance. Admitting his "want of qualification" in that he had no academic experience, Barker pledged to seek diligently for the funds to advance the university to the "very fore-front of the educational in-

stitutions of the country." The board submitted the new president's name to the governor before he got around to accepting Patterson's six-month-old letter of resignation on June 16.

Barker's admission of want of experience was well taken. Presumably he had learned something about the university as a member of the Board of Trustees and should have been under no illusions about the nature of the presidency. He had attractive personal qualities. His appearance was impressive, and he carried himself with dignity. He had an equable disposition, and students liked him, whereas they had stood in awe of Patterson—which accounts for their tendency to satirize Patterson but not Barker. The new president also enjoyed sporting events and admitted the desirability of friendliness toward athletics.

But Barker's open, trusting nature led him to underestimate the potential for trouble built into the terms of Patterson's retirement. The former president had virtually dictated them, and the trustees, Barker included, had blithely acquiesced. Perhaps the board's most insensitive concession was granting permission for Patterson to reside in the president's home on campus, at nominal rent, while President and Mrs. Barker occupied an apartment in the girl's dormitory. Given Patterson's assertive personality, the board should have foreseen that such an arrangement was an invitation to meddling. Yet even in 1917, when an investigating committee recommended Patterson's removal from the house, the board rejected the advice—perhaps because of the purchase of what would become after that year the new president's home, Maxwell Place. So Patterson stayed on until his death in 1922, and, for no discernible reason, his brother, Walter K., then a downtown banker, was allowed to live there until his death in 1932.

The plans for Pence Hall (above), built to house civil engineering and physics, were drawn by Merry L. Pence, head of the physics department, according to his daughter Sallie. Dean Paul Anderson and Leon Frankel of Mechanical Engineering were the architects for Kastle Hall (left). This picture shows only the south section, first known as the New Chemistry Building. Kastle Hall was not completed until the mid-1920s, and the original plans were much altered to produce the final building.

State College became State University without a central library on campus. Not until he was contemplating retirement did Patterson seek funds for a library from his friend Andrew Carnegie, who contributed $26,000 for the

building. When it was dedicated on November 24, 1909, it became the second Carnegie Library in Lexington, the first being the public library on Second Street. It stood about a hundred yards behind the Administration Building. Of no

distinctive architectural style, it nevertheless was an aesthetically pleasing little building that deserved to survive (but did not) the demolitions of the mid-1960s.

When Barker assumed office on January 1, 1911, the university seemed poised to move ahead. Its building needs had been met for the time being with the recent construction of Pence Hall for physics and civil engineering, the new Carnegie Library, the first portion of Kastle Hall for chemistry, and a recent extension of the six-year-old (second) Experiment Station building.

The statistical measurements of growth during Barker's tenure gave satisfaction. In his last year, 1916-17, the university enrolled 986 students, nearly double the number of his first year. The annual number of degrees awarded increased by almost 50 percent, from 104 in 1911 to 153 in 1917. In the same period the size of the faculty and staff grew from 101 to 163. The university added 95 acres of land, most of them for the Experiment Station Farm. A strategic purchase in 1917 consisted of the thirteen-acre Mulligan tract between the campus and Rose Street and from Winslow Street to Washington Avenue. On it stood Maxwell Place, the Mulligan home built in 1871, which was to be refurbished for use as the president's home. The university's income, too, doubled during Barker's incumbency, reaching the sum of $543,000 in his last year.

These figures were impressive only in comparison with the university's own past, not in comparison with the land grant institutions in neighboring states, especially to the north and west. Changes and improvements had indeed occurred at State University, but rival institutions were growing at a faster pace.

The library was a case in point. Though a bookish man, Patterson never pushed hard to acquire books or a library building until Andrew Carnegie came to his aid with an unusual gift of money for a university building. Before that, university books were scattered among departmental libraries or in faculty offices. They were not available to students until 1912, when they were gathered into the Carnegie Library and catalogued by the school's first librarian, Margaret I. King. Only then, and because of Barker's intervention, were books allowed to circulate among students.

Barker's was a more enlightened view about the place of a library in a university than any Patterson had expressed. In Barker's first year the university began budgetary allocations for book purchases and librarians' pay. By 1917 the library had added 34,000 volumes, four times its holdings in 1908, when Patterson had proudly called the scattered volumes a collection "for historical and literary research." Charming as the Carnegie Library building was, it was too small, and its inadequacy became more pronounced with each passing year of the twenty that went by before a new one was constructed.

Upon becoming a university, the institution moved to strengthen graduate education, which had been increasing in the last years of State College. It had granted master's degrees since 1876, by 1910 a total of 123, all but 19 in the previous decade. Against this background it seemed appropriate for the university to continue the momentum. To give to graduate studies stronger supervision than the existing graduate committee provided, Alexander St. Clair Mackenzie was appointed dean of the new Graduate School in 1912. A professor of English and one of the few publishing scholars on the faculty, he was an exemplary choice. But when Mackenzie left the university in 1916 and a supervisory committee replaced him, graduate work fell into the doldrums until the deanship and the Graduate School were revived in 1924. Not for nearly another decade would the university authorize doctoral programs.

Alexander St. Clair Mackenzie was the first dean of graduate studies, serving from 1912 to 1916.

Compared with those in earlier photos, this group of about half the 1912 faculty and staff looks more relaxed; some members even appear downright lighthearted. Barker's presidency set a new tone for the campus and faculty.

The original faculty of the department of journalism consisted of Enoch Grehan (B.A., Kentucky University, 1894) and Marjorie McLaughlin (B.A., State College, 1903). Both were working on Lexington newspapers when the university employed them. Grehan was professor and head of the department until his death in 1937. "Miss Margie," an instructor, remained a campus personality until her retirement in 1951.

At the undergraduate level, however, improvements and enlargements continued to take place. The size of the faculty and staff increased from 82 to 163 during the eight-year life of State University. The College of Arts and Science added two new departments, journalism and one combining philosophy and psychology. Enoch Grehan of the Lexington *Herald* went to Columbia University's school of journalism to prepare for the inauguration of the journalism department and for the handling of the university's printing. He and his colleague Marguerite McLaughlin, also an experienced journalist, were interested in providing enlarged opportunities for

THE KENTUCKY KERNEL

State University of Kentucky

VOL. VIII. LEXINGTON, KENTUCKY, SEPT. 16, 1915. No. 1.

University Begins Year With Bright Prospects

More Than 900 Matriculate on First Two Days of School and Many More are Expected Before End of Week.

NUMEROUS CHANGES ARE MADE IN FACULTY

Whn the doors of Buell Armory were formally thrown open Monday morning for the beginning of the forty-seventh annual session of the University, a large crowd was waiting to matriculate, and it was after 6 o'clock Tuesday night before the registration ceased. A total of 918 were registered in the two days and this number is expected to be considerably augmented before the end of the week.

The matriculation was carried on very systematically, very little trouble being experienced by the students. After matriculation, the students were able to find out about their courses, classes, et cetera, from the representatives of the various colleges who were seated around the walls.

Various changes have been made in several departments, both in courses and faculty. The College of Agriculture has added courses in vegetable gardening and in floriculture. The greenhouses and gardens at the Experiment Station will be used by the students this year more than ever before. Two additions have been made to the faculty of this college. N. R. Elliot, from Ohio State University, takes the position made vacant by the resignation or Fred Hofman, who accepted a position with the Bureau of Markets Department, of Washington, D. C., and Dr. Philip L. Blumenthal, graduate of this University and of Yale, has accepted a position as chemist at the Experiment Station.

Candidates for degrees in this department who have not done practical farming work, will be required to work on the farm at least two summers before they can graduate.

The College of Law has added a requirement for entrance that all students under twenty-one years of age must have one year of university work. In this department two additions have been made to the faculty Reuben B. Hutchcraft, Jr., graduate of Transylvania College and of the Harvard Law School, will be instructor and George DuRelle, of Louisville, will deliver a course of lectures on "Federal Jurisdiction and Procedure."

In the Arts and Science College additions have been made in the Chemistry, English and Journalism Departments. J. R. Mitchell, of Westminister College; William H. Staebner, of Clark College, and A. H. Waltt, of Massachusetts Technical Institute, have been added to the Chemistry Department as professors of elementary

(Continued on Page 3)

LETTER SENT SENIORS WARNS AGAINST HAZING

Freshman Hair Not to be Cut This Year, Is the Faculty Rule

On September 6 a letter was sent by the President of the University to each male member of the Senior class, and one to the parents of each male member, emphasizing the seriousness of the offense of hazing, which includes hair-cutting, and stating the penalty for any infraction of the anti-hazing rule. The letter addressed to the students follows:

Lexington, Ky., Sept. 6, 1915.
"My Dear Young Friend:—

"At the coming session of the University, you will be in the Senior class.

"The object of this letter is to call your attention to the fact that the faculty has passed a stringent rule against hazing of any kind, and especially against that form of hazing which consists in cutting the Freshmen's hair. I also wish to remind you that, last year, when certain young men in the dormitories were reinstated for the offense of hazing, it was done upon the promise that hereafter all sorts of hazing would be banished from the campus. That was the contract signed by all the students in the dormitories.

"Frequently, when students have gotten into trouble in the University and been punished, they have appealed to me, as President of the University, on the grounds they did not know the existence of the law for the breach of which they were punished. Thus far, I have always helped them out of trouble, but having obligated myself to the faculty to carry out this rule, it will be my duty to see that the law against hazing is enforced next session.

"I hope you will return to school in good health and spirits, and with the full determination to assist me in the enforcement of all lawful discipline on the campus and to uphold my hand in everything for the good of "State."

"I hope you will not consider this in any way, a threat, but that you will feel that it has come from my heart and for your benefit.

"Hoping to see you soon on the campus, I am

"HENRY S. BARKER,

MRS. JAS. K. PATTERSON DIES AT CAMPUS HOME

Beloved Wife of President Emeritus Passes Away Friday

RESOLUTIONS PASSED

The many students of the University, members of the faculty, officers of the administration, friends and acquaintances were grieved to hear of the death of Mrs. Lucelia W. Patterson, which occurred at her residence on the University campus last Friday afternoon at 3 o'clock. Bronchitis, contracted a few weeks ago, was the cause of her death. Mrs. Patterson is survived by her husband, Dr. James K. Patterson, president emeritus of State University, and by a sister, Mrs. Lucy R. Yost, of Greenville, Ky. She was 80 years old.

The funeral services were held at the Patterson home on the University campus Sunday afternoon at 3 o'clock, the Rev. Edwin Muller, pastor of the First Presbyterian Church, and the Rev. Dr. Charles Lee Reynolds, pastor of the Second Presbyterian Church, conducting the services. The interment took place in the Patterson mausoleum in the Lexington cemetery.

The loss of one of Kentucky's most noble women was deeply lamented through the local press, and in resolutions adopted by the Alumnae Club and the faculty of State University Saturday afternoon as follows:

"Whereas, it has pleased an all-wise Providence to remove from our midst Lucelia Wing Patterson, the beloved wife of James K. Patterson, president emeritus of State University;

"Therefore, be it resolved by the faculty of the State University that we extend to Doctor Patterson our sincere and heart-felt sympathy in this sad hour of his bereavement.

"For many years his stay and helpmate, she brought into his life the inspiration and charm of a gentle womanliness, the hope and steadfastness of purpose of a Christian character.

"Gentle, kindly, patient, actuated only by noble purposes, a gentlewoman by birth and education, she left an abiding impress for good upon the lives of many generations of students, and into the atmosphere of

(Continued on Page 2)

STAFF MEETING.

The first meeting of the staff of The Kentucky Kernel will be held Friday afternoon at 3:30 o'clock in the Journalism Department rooms in the basement of the Main Building. Plans for the year will be discussed and details of the system will be worked out. It is absolutely imperative that each member of the staff attend this meeting unless prevented by something unavoidable. This is the most important staff meeting for the year.

J. FRANKLIN CORN, Editor.

Blue and White Team Has Best Prospects in Years

Strongest Preliminary Offerings Yet Made For Football Work on New Barker Field—Number of 200-Pounders Trying For the Team.

DEDICARY CONTEST IS SET FOR OCTOBER 2.

```
WILDCAT FIGHTS, 1915.

Oct. 2—Butler College, at Lexington.
Oct. 9—Earlham College, at Lexington.
Oct. 16—Mississippi A. & M. College, at Columbus, Miss.
Oct. 23—University of the South (Sewanee), at Lexington.
Oct. 30—University of Cincinnati, at Lexington.
Nov. 6—University of Louisville, at Louisville.
Nov. 13—Purdue University, at Lexington.
Nov. 26 (Thanksgiving)—University of Tennessee, at Lexington.
```

"It seems to me that only a very bad run of luck could prevent State from having one of the best football teams she has ever had," said Dr. Tigert, the popular University coach, familiarly referred to among the student body as "Tige," the other evening after coming in from the new Barker Stadium with his large squad of prospective Wildcats.

"Everything points to a bright year," continued the "long logician." "We have a splendid field—undoubtedly one of the best in the South. The material at hand is excellent; the athletic committee is backing us more than ever before and besides all these, it seems to me that the student body is taking greater interest than in former years."

Track suits and scant football outfits are in evidence every afternoon among the forty or fifty warriors who are braving the spell of warm weather and gamely running down punts, kicking, passing and the other preliminaries Coach Tigert and his assistant, "Squirrely" Tuttle are putting the men through. The University and Coach Tigert are fortunate in securing the aid of Tuttle and Jim Park, who will arrive soon from St. Louis to take up his duties at Kentucky State, who for the past four years have been responsible for many a Wildcat victory on the gridiron as well as in other branches of athletics. Park at quarter and Tuttle as halfback have probably never been surpassed in their respective positions on the eleven and certainly never before as all around athletes and students.

Everyone is familiar with the winning powers which the head coach

(Continued on Page 3)

WILD CATS MAKE GOOD IN PROFESSIONAL BALL

Park, Thomas, Reed and Wright Play Season With Lexington

PARK WITH ST. LOUIS

(Special Dispatch to the Kentucky Kernel.)

PHILADELPHIA, Pa., Sept. 14.— James Park, former Kentucky State University athlete, of the St. Louis Browns, won his third successive game, defeating the local team here today, score 12 to 4. Park allowed only four hits and struck out three men.

The ability of Kentucky State Wildcats to make good outside of college amateur circles has been amply demonstrated during the past summer by the records of "Jim" Park, Ad Thomas, "Rasty" Wright, and "Biscuit" Reed, all of whom have been playing professional baseball this season, and who have decidedly made good. All of them were members of the Lexington Ohio State League team, which was a contender in both of split-season races in that league, and the K. S. U. boys were among the best in the whole circuit.

Paul Gossage, the well-known pitcher, who was a student in the Law Department last year, but was prevented from playing on the University team because of his professional record, spent the summer as a member of the Charlotte (N. C.) team in the North Carolina League.

"Jim" Park was purchased by the St. Louis American League team for a price said to be one of the largest ever paid for an Ohio State League player and reported to them during the latter part of August. On September 7 he pitched his first game in the majors against the Cleveland team, opposing him and as was expected of him won the game, by the score of 4 to 1. Not only that, but the game went to eleven innings, and "Jim" was responsible for the victory by slamming out a two-bagger in the eleventh and driving in two men with the winning runs. During the game he struck out six men and allowed only two bases on balls. This remarkable

(Continued on Page 2)

Students returning for the fall semester of 1915 were greeted by the first issue of the new weekly student newspaper, the Kentucky Kernel. The volume number, VIII, established continuity with its predecessor, the Idea, begun in 1908. The Kernel therefore had a history—and a future, for it is still published, now five days a week during the regular school year.

students to write for publication. In 1915, as a weekly campus newspaper, the *Kentucky Kernel* began its career.

Expansion of the administration also reflected the change from college to university. Deans proliferated, including the new position of dean of men, and the offices of registrar, librarian, and business agent became steadily more important.

At State University under Barker, the atmosphere was lighter and less oppressive than at Patterson's State College. One refreshing change was the enlarged opportunities for student self-expression. The *Kentuckian* yearbook, replacing the old *Echoes,* had begun in the last year of State College and at once became well established. The student newspaper, the *Kentucky Kernel,* immediately acquired status. The names of *Kentucky Law Journal* and *The Transit* suggest their professional character as outlets for the creative efforts of law and engineering students.

A five-year experiment with student government that ended in 1917 was intended to serve as an honor system, with an elected council to handle allegations of misconduct. The plan did not work and is remembered only as a forerunner of a venture in student government in the early 1920s that did endure.

Student desire for a richer social life found freer and more varied outlets than ever before. Barker Hall accommodated indoor sports—notably bas-

Many student clubs were short-lived, ceasing once their members graduated. Such was the Mandolin Club of 1910-11 (below), a ten-member string ensemble that grew from this foursome. Another group was the 1912 Bachelor's Club (right), debonair men-about-town who dressed in the height of fashion; some of these dandies had to use buttonhooks to get into their well-polished shoes. The club's photogenic members include (but not in order) W.A. Stanfill, J.S. Golden, N.W. Utley, Jr., R.W. Tinsley, Hugh Kelley, S.L. Pannell, and J.B. Thomas.

OPPOSITE: The student government association, comprising all enrolled students, was created in 1912 at the insistence of President Barker. Members elected the executive committee, which heard cheating and misconduct charges. The constitution required that the representation of each class include at least one woman. In the early 1920s, a greatly amended student government was reconstituted after a six-year lapse—but not as an honor system.

President of the first executive committee, shown here, was W.C. Harrison, D.D. Felix was vice president, and Jessie Milton Jones was secretary. The senior representatives were Addie Lee Dean, R.W. Tinsley, and W.H. Jaegle; juniors, Lucille Gastineau, R.H. Thomas and F.J. Forsythe; sophomores, Pauline Hank and P.D. Brown; and freshmen, Elsie Speck and J.W. Wesson.

OPPOSITE TOP: The Henry Clay Law Society in 1912 included one woman, Helen Louise Whittinghill, a special student rather than a degree candidate but apparently regarded highly enough to be admitted to this prestigious organization.

OPPOSITE BOTTOM: Faculty of the College of Mechanical Engineering in 1910 invited their back-fence neighbor, Judge J.H. Mulligan, to an event unthinkable today—a departmental smoker. This photo shows another such social occasion for pipe-smoking mechanical engineering juniors, again hosted by Dean Anderson (second row, extreme left).

RIGHT: The campus in 1911 could boast neither vending machines nor a grill, and students either had to leave campus for the nearest soda fountain or patronize peddlers such as Phil or another wagon that went around selling bakery goods.

ketball for women and men, wrestling, and gymnastics—as well as dances and other indoor recreation. The eight fraternities and six sororities, occupying nearby rented houses, introduced students to a new style of living and varied social activities. Some student societies, sponsored or sanctioned by regular academic units, served both academic and social purposes. One of the best-known and most highly regarded was the Strollers, a drama group composed of students and townspeople. After 1911 it presented plays on and off campus and in other towns. The Strollers, said the *Kentuckian*, were "self-supporting and self-directed," and indeed the group was always solvent. Like drama, the band, orchestra, and glee club were extracurricular activities rather than parts of the official program, but the experience in self-direction was a valuable part of the university experience.

The literary societies remained active, and the debate and oratory they promoted were favorite kinds of intercollegiate and intramural competition. Students eager for excitement traveled by train to neighboring colleges to cheer on their

Replacing the annual freshman-sophomore flag rushes beginning in 1913, the tug-of-war across Clifton Pond may have been less threatening to life and limb but engendered just as much temporary rivalry between the two classes. This October 1914 tug saw the freshmen triumph. But, with everyone given a half-holiday for the event, even some of the sophomores probably thought it a glorious day.

debaters and orators. A march from the Georgetown train station to the college, for instance, was an exuberant display of boastful defiance, and the march back would be high-spirited or crestfallen, depending on the circumstances. Forensic luminaries were campus heroes, none more acclaimed than Virgil Chapman, a law student known on campus and in Lexington as the "silver-tongued orator." Like their predecessors of State College and State University times, University of Kentucky debaters continued to excel against competitors.

State University inherited the tradition of the flag rush, an annual brawl between freshmen and sophomores that took place each October around the flagpole in front of Main Building. It was a dress occasion for townspeople and faculty wives, but President Barker, aware that the rush was becoming too rough, persuaded the class presidents to call it off in 1911. The next year a tug-of-war with a cable stretched across Clifton Pond took its place. That may have been a less dangerous contest, but one year the victors paraded through the downtown streets with the cable and on West Third Street, in view of the Transylvania students, got in the way of a streetcar. One student died from his injuries.

Class warfare, like the hazing of freshmen and fraternity initiates, was not unique to State University, only representative of a national practice with remote origins.

Elizabeth "Bess" Hayden (B.A. 1916) was a campus personality and—of special note—was captain of the girls' basketball team and "[threw] a ball like a man."

In the State University period the football teams laid the foundation for a winning tradition, though it never developed as a long-term feature of the institution's athletic history. From 1908 through 1915 every football season was a winning one. In 1908 the team went 9-1, losing only to North Carolina A&M and winning over Tennessee and Illinois. In the 7-2 season of 1912 it beat North Carolina, Tulane, Tennessee, and Ohio University. By this time State University was getting too big for the KIAA and was looking for more prestigious opponents. From 1913 to 1915 its only Kentucky opponent was Louisville, while it played Tennessee every year and, among other schools, Illinois, Mississippi A&M, and Purdue. Vanderbilt first played in Lexington in 1916 at the dedication of Stoll Field—and spoiled the festivities by beating the home team

45-0. That was the first season under the new name of the University of Kentucky, and it was not a good omen. Though the season was a winning one, it was the last of a string that had begun in 1903, the longest winning streak in the university's football history. Centre, beaten 68-0 in 1916, remained an exception among Kentucky colleges in playing UK regularly through 1929. The trend was apparent: the university was finding its place in regional competition, and the end of World War I saw it looking southward in athletics.

Basketball continued to lag behind for several years. The schedule for 1913-14 included two games each with the Louisville YMCA and the Ashland YMCA; not until the next year did State University begin to play regularly with its neighbors Tennessee and Vanderbilt. Basketball

Kentucky was on a roll. With a 7-2 record in 1912, the football team hadn't had a losing season since 1902, nor would it again until 1917. Note the iron goalposts, the bleacher fans to the rear, and the houses on the north side of Winslow Street where the Coliseum now stands.

James "Turkey" Park, State University's all-around athlete—captain and quarterback in football and a highly capable pitcher-hitter in baseball.

remained a January-February sport until 1924, the year the Alumni Gym opened. From 1909 through 1916, State University had six winning seasons and two losing ones, playing less formidable opponents in basketball than in football. In both sports State University played in antiquated settings, before wooden bleachers in football and in a crackerbox gymnasium in basketball. Not for another eight years would the teams play in settings more congenial to their rising ambitions.

Before UK athletics obtained wider recognition, in the days when All-American teams were made up mostly of players from the Ivy League, the best-known State University athlete was James Park (B.A. 1915), who excelled in football, basketball, and especially baseball. He earned ten letters in sports. A mathematics major and president of his senior class, he went on to pitch in major league baseball for five years, three of them with the St. Louis Browns of the American League. Between seasons he attended the UK law school and coached the basketball team to an 8-6 season in 1915-16. After receiving his law degree in 1920, he practiced in Lexington and remained a loyal supporter of UK athletics.

$\mathbf{A}$s State University grew larger and its programs more diverse, students spread their efforts into more varied fields, but no patterns emerged among the careers of outstanding alumni except for the continued prominence of engineering graduates. Herman Lee Donovan (B.A. 1914) was one of the few who went into academic life, becoming president of his alma mater in 1941. Mervin Joe Kelly (M.S. 1915) went on for a doctoral degree at the University of Chicago, joined Bell Laboratories in 1925, rose to the presidency, and won recognition as one of the nation's leading industrial scientists. Margaret Ingels, the first woman to graduate in engineering at the university, joined the Carrier Engineering Corporation in 1917, where another alumnus, J. Irwin Lyle, was president. Ingels specialized in air conditioning, and when she retired in Lexington in 1953 was perhaps the foremost woman nationally in the growing field.

Virgil Chapman staked out the direction of his future while making a notable career in the university. He entered the law college in 1913, took time off along the way to practice politics in Frankfort, and returned in 1917 for his senior year. His student record was brilliant: he was junior class orator, president of his senior class (the first to be elected unanimously), editor-in-chief of the *Kentucky Law Journal*, chairman of the Board of Control of the *Kentucky Kernel*, and instructor of law in his final year. Elected to the U.S. House of Representatives in 1924, he served there—except for a two year interval—until he was elected to the United States Senate in 1948. He died in Washington, D.C., in a 1951 automobile accident.

While still a freshman, Chapman earned campus notoriety for something that might later have been seen as a claim to fame. During the night of January 28, 1914, in the hazing season, he was roused out of bed in the old dorm and forced to run twice around Main Building, clad only in his socks. That performance makes him the original UK streaker.

In his senior year in law, Virgil Chapman, known as the "silver-tongued orator," was the big man on campus.

OPPOSITE: Three State University alumni: Margaret Ingels, Herman Lee Donovan, and Mervin Joe Kelly.

On March 15, 1916, the legislature, without stating a reason, changed the name of State University to the University of Kentucky. Nevertheless, the next fifteen months belong to the history of State University. The leading event was an examination of Barker's presidency by a committee of trustees whose report in June 1917 caused Barker to resign at once. Only then, with a new president to be sought, did the history of the University of Kentucky as such properly begin.

The immediate cause of the investigation was Barker's courageous recommendation to merge the three engineering colleges into one. Vested interests and personal ambitions took sides on the question of a single deanship, and as factions formed, various resentments came into the open: alleged salary differentials among faculty members, departmental rivalries over money allocations, a general perception of the need for more generous funding of the university, and, specifically, inadequate leadership in the College of Agriculture. Naturally, the blame for all of these conditions came back to the president. Some persons in and outside the university thought they perceived political hostility against Barker going back to his time as judge in the Court of Appeals.

To resolve the turmoil, in January 1917 the governor, as chairman of the Board of Trustees, appointed a committee to examine the situation in engineering and look into the complaints heard from faculty, students, and some of the public. With such a wide area to explore, the investigating committee engaged three out-of-state educators as an expert survey committee to report in June. The educators subjected the institution to the most searching scrutiny it had

The Golden Jubilee of October 12-14, 1916, celebrated the fiftieth anniversary of the opening of classes on the Woodlands-Ashland campus. To most people in attendance, the day's crowning events were the ceremonies dedicating Stoll Field, in honor of trustee Richard C. Stoll, and the football game with Vanderbilt. The State College team did the "courteous" thing and gave the victory to the visitors, 45-0. Patterson and Barker (center) were, of course, both in attendance. Thomas Hunt Morgan is at left in the light suit. The date of passage of the 1865 statute — February 22 — is still officially known as Founders Day, but since 1944 the university's founding year has been moved from 1866 back to 1865.

ever undergone; the trustees' committee accepted the educators' report; and the full board accepted all but one of its committee's recommendations—the one for the removal of Patterson from the president's home.

The report was frank and constructive. While it spoke kindly of Barker as a person, recognizing the plight in which the board placed him when it gave Patterson large opportunities to make a nuisance of himself, it nevertheless said that Barker should not have been appointed in the first place because, lacking the qualifying background, he did not know what needed doing when he became president. Too many faculty members were underqualified and too few were doing original research. Professors were underpaid, required to teach excessive loads and perform too many administrative chores, and given too little weight in university affairs.

The report also noted problems with facilities and administration. The men's dormitories should be condemned as "public nuisances," and

The commencement of 1917 was the last of President Barker's administration. After handing out 153 diplomas like this one to the first class to graduate from the "University of Kentucky," Barker met with the Board of Trustees to receive the report of its investigating committee, which was critical of Barker's qualifications for the presidency. He resigned at once. The occasion was, properly speaking, the termination of State University, although the new name already appeared on diplomas.

The Golden Jubilee included alumni reunions and the conferring of honorary degrees. Among the fifteen recipients were Thomas Hunt Morgan, James Lane Allen, and Henry Watterson. The Main Street parade included this senior section looking forward to receiving diplomas like the one on the previous page.

other buildings demanded renovation. The College of Agriculture needed tighter organization: the dean's threefold responsibilities for the Experiment Station, the teaching college, and especially the Extension Service lacked strong, clear definition. As Barker had recommended, the three engineering colleges should be consolidated under a dean brought in from the outside. Finally (actually, the committee's first recommendation), the incumbent president should be asked to resign within a year and a joint board-faculty committee should be appointed to search for a successor.

President Barker resigned at once, not wishing to accept what in effect would be a year's terminal pay. The search committee made a recommendation on August 15, and a new president took office a month later. There can be few other instances in American higher education of such speed and, as it turned out, such effectiveness in decisionmaking as UK's in the first nine months of 1917. Barker's cooperation was one of the reasons. The history of the University of Kentucky could begin.

Chapter 4

The University of Kentucky
1916-1956

Above: Frank LeRond McVey, president of the University of Kentucky from 1917 to 1940. McVey's first wife died after their move to Kentucky. In December 1923, Mary Frances Jewell (opposite), former instructor of English and more recently dean of women, became the president's second wife.

Maxwell Place was new as the president's home, and it was open to the second Mrs. McVey to determine its place on the campus. President McVey, having accomplished many of the reconstructive tasks he had found waiting for him in 1917, fell in with her ambition to make the president's home a center of campus life, and Maxwell Place soon established itself as one of the great traditions of UK, remembered most fondly by alumni who were students in the 1920s and '30s.

The transition from State University to University of Kentucky lasted a year and a half. It began on March 15, 1916, when the legislature bestowed the new name, continued through the unsettling events of the next fifteen months, and ended on August 15, 1917, when the Board of Trustees unanimously approved the appointment of Frank LeRond McVey. The new president took office on September 14.

McVey's credentials met in every respect the criteria the investigating committee had specified. Moreover, he possessed the personal and physical attributes of an ideal university president of that time—tall and distinguished in appearance, friendly in manner but properly reserved. He was a native of Ohio and had earned a doctoral degree in economics from Yale. On the faculty of the University of Minnesota he had chaired the Minnesota Tax Commission and had published scholarly books and articles. As president of the University of North Dakota from 1909 to 1917, he made a lasting impression and acquired national stature. Indeed, had he bided his time, a presidency more prestigious than Kentucky's might have come his way during the predictable postwar expansion of higher education. But against the background of the investigation he may have perceived the determination of the board and the state to move the university forward.

On September 19, 1917, the day McVey first presided over a board meeting, the *Kentucky Kernel* expressed sentiments that must have pleased him. The university, it said, was entering upon a new era. The dissensions and troubles of recent months were cleared up; the new president would find those about him ready to follow firm, competent leadership.

A view of Maxwell Place (the former Mulligan home) during the McVeys' residence there. The house had been renovated before the McVeys moved in, but much remained to be done to the exterior when Frances Jewell became chatelaine.

The investigating committee of 1917 was horrified by the state of disrepair on campus, including such sights as this in the chapel on the second floor of the Administration Building. When President McVey took office a few months later, he at once set in motion a general renovation and cleanup.

It was a banner day for the university in March 1918 when Governor A.O. Stanley signed the bill appropriating an additional $200,000 a year for UK. While President McVey, trustee Richard Stoll, and business agent David H. Peak looked on at the signing in Frankfort, students back in Lexington paraded down Limestone to Main Street to celebrate the occasion.

McVey began his administration under good omens. A prior commitment to the war effort kept him in Washington until January, but he returned to Lexington each month to attend to university business. During that time he recruited the man he wanted as dean of the College of Agriculture: Thomas Poe Cooper, the director of the North Dakota Experiment Station. Within a year Cooper achieved the long-desired unity among the three divisions of agriculture and established a pattern for all subsequent deans of the college.

During the autumn of nonresidency, McVey also carried out another important recommendation of the investigating committee by drawing up a constitution for the university. Its most important provision created a Faculty Senate with authority over the curriculum as well as "matters involving general University policy." In addition, the constitution established a sabbatical leave policy to encourage faculty research and other scholarly activities.

In March 1918 the General Assembly added to the euphoria at the university with a permanent grant of an additional $200,000 each year. On receipt of the eagerly awaited news from Frankfort, the student body paraded exuberantly along Limestone and Main Streets and paid deserved tribute to a Lexington legislator, William F. Klair, for piloting the bill through the legislature. This epochal appropriation inaugurated a decade of growth in state support for the university.

Turning to an old problem, McVey secured the appointment of Paul Anderson, incumbent dean

Billy Klair (far left, 1874-1937), a longtime member of the General Assembly and a power in the Democratic party, was one of the best friends UK ever had.

Thomas Poe Cooper (left) unified the tripartite division of the work in agriculture on becoming dean of the College of Agriculture, head of the Extension Service, and director of the Experiment Station. He was primarily responsible for expansion of the university farm in the 1920s to nearly 600 acres. Cooper also served as acting president while a successor to McVey was sought in 1940. He retired in 1951.

of the Mechanical Engineering College, to the deanship of the consolidated College of Engineering. No one doubted Anderson's ability or his effective promotion of the interests of engineering, and he was popular among the students. But some questioned the propriety of his interest in an architectural firm, and some disliked his natty way of dressing and of driving big, flashy automobiles, not to mention his eagerness to have his picture taken (generally satisfied by Louis Nollau, who was often conveniently at hand with camera and tripod).

While the university was arranging for its new order, World War I was upsetting the old order of the world about it. The school acted quickly to help students once the nation entered the war, providing convenient terms for academic credits for those whose education had been interrupted by military service. In 1918 the university contracted with the government for the training of military personnel in technical skills. Between May and November three detachments of regulars went through training courses on the campus. Barker Hall's Buell Armory became a workshop for truck maintenance and repair. Male students entered the Students' Army Training Corps (SATC) or a naval training unit.

The campus became a combined military post and academic institution. Faculty continued their regular teaching duties and, when qualified, assisted in teaching the military units or entered government service. The regular soldiers were housed at the trotting track on South Broadway until hastily constructed barracks were ready at the east end of Stoll Field, but they were hardly in use when the war ended. By that time the regulars and the SATC had been combined into

The first of three contingents to receive special military training at UK arrived in May 1918. Mainly from Tennessee, these recruits marched to the campus from Union Station on Main Street, an architectural gem demolished in 1960. Among the skills they would learn were truck maintenance and repair.

In October 1918 the worldwide flu epidemic struck the university campus, and emergency measures were instituted. Barker Hall gymnasium became an infirmary, *though the most seriously ill were taken to local hospitals.*

a single unit, the National Training Detachment. In the fall of 1918 the influenza epidemic struck the campus, and the gymnasium was turned into an infirmary. Five trainees died in the epidemic.

All of this activity quieted quickly after the war ended. By December 21 demobilization had left the university once again a civilian institution. As a land grant institution, however, it still had to offer military training; henceforth this would be done under the newly established Reserve Officer Training Corps. In the life of the campus, ROTC played an important part, first as a requirement for male students and after 1963 as an elective. Women could enroll beginning in 1966.

The university was proud of its contribution to the war effort. The war had hardly ended when a campaign was undertaken to raise money for a fitting memorial to the 1,007 students, alumni, and faculty who had been in service, of whom 8 were killed in action and 11 died from accident or illness. The memorial, a decade later, was the much photographed auditorium building, Memorial Hall.

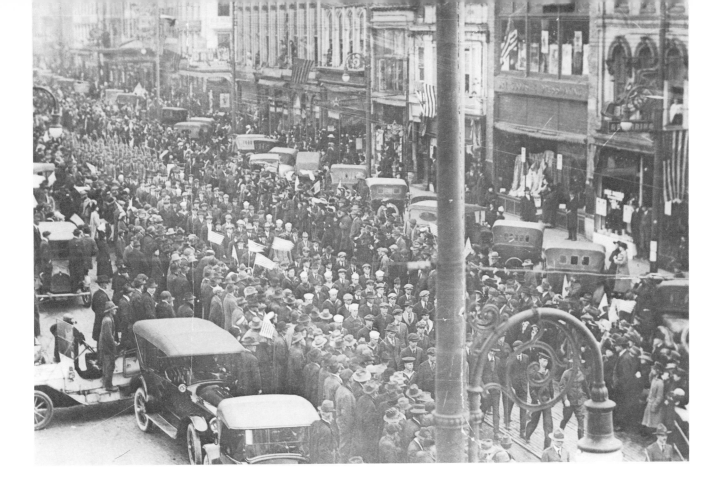

The Armistice Day parade on Main Street on November 11, 1918, marking the end of World War I, included army and navy units from the university.

Between the end of World War I and the depth of the Great Depression in 1932, enrollment in UK steadily increased to 4,992, creating a need for additional classrooms and dormitories, a larger library, more laboratories, dining facilities, and athletic and recreational accommodations. On the periphery of the campus and south and east of the farm, land purchases expanded the campus and farm right up to 1932.

The land along Winslow Street was the logical place for improvement and expansion of the athletic facilities already located there. The ground was tilled, filled, and graded in prepara-

tion for a planned gymnasium at the northwest corner and a football stadium on the eastern portion, now extended to Rose Street. The football field, already named for Richard C. Stoll, would be surrounded by a running track.

The original architect's drawing shows a handsome horseshoe-shaped stadium with the open end toward Limestone Street. In that age of large new university football facilities, the planned seating capacity of 35,000, however impressive locally, was a bit modest considering that UK teams had had only three losing seasons from 1903 to 1924. Despite that history of football suc-

The earliest building on the quadrangle was Bradley Hall (at right, in photo at left), built in 1921. This view shows, from left, Breckinridge and Kinkead halls, both built in 1930. Not until 1949 was the quadrangle filled in on the Washington Avenue side with the construction of Bowman Hall.

BELOW: Wildcat football teams played in McLean Stadium from its completion in 1924 through the season of 1972, when it was replaced by Commonwealth Stadium. The original stadium seated only 15,000; the expansion of 1948 increased its capacity to 35,000.

cess, nerve failed and money was sufficient only for concrete stands seating 15,000 spectators on the long sides of the field. Opened for the 1924 season, the stadium was named for Price McLean, a Lexington engineering student who had been injured fatally in the game with Cincinnati the year before. The gym was named Alumni Gymnasium in acknowledgment of the contributions toward its construction from alumni and the public. At last the university had a place to play basketball which, when it opened in 1924, could accommodate the entire student body (then a little under 2,000) and about 1,500 faculty and townspeople as well.

These new facilities and the ambitions they symbolized emphasized the continuing tendency to cultivate athletic competition with schools larger than the Kentucky colleges. The university became a member of the Southern Conference, which was reorganized in 1933 as the Southeastern Conference. Its prominence revealed the inadequacy of the 1920s facilities, but not until after World War II were moves made to improve them. Yet in a gym seating 3,500 and in a stadium seating 15,000, Adolph Rupp and Bear Bryant began the careers that ended in coaching immortality.

Meanwhile, up on the hill, academic space needs were being attended to. Internal rearrangements accommodated new administrative offices and a cafeteria in the Administration Building. The older and newer men's dorms, renamed White Hall and Neville Hall, were converted into classroom and office buildings. In 1921 Bradley Hall opened as the first side of a planned dormitory quadrangle at Rose Street and Washington Avenue. The second and third parts, Breckinridge and Kinkead Halls, were completed in 1930, and in 1949 the open side on Washington Avenue was filled in by Bowman Hall. At the op-

This 1928 flood damaged coaches' offices in Alumni Gym, built in 1924. The post office, also housed in the building, was damaged and soon thereafter moved to the newly completed McVey Hall.

Memorial Hall (1929), the long awaited memorial to UK students, alumni, and faculty who served in World War I, was destined to become the most photographed building on the campus. The front view was dominated by the tower and a Corinthian-columned porch. The Greek theater behind it was a standard feature of campus beautification in American colleges of the 1920s.

posite corner of the campus in the area marked out for women's dormitories, Boyd Hall came into use in 1925.

Construction went on continually about the campus for the rest of the decade. On Winslow Street (after 1926, Euclid Avenue), just east of the women's dorms, the old Consolidated Baptist church was converted into the Romany Theater in 1923. Soon it was enlarged to house music and art as well as drama and renamed the Guignol Theater. The expansion of Kastle Hall in the mid-1920s enabled the chemistry department to reunite and freed the old Experiment Station building for the College of Law. In front of Kastle Hall, on the west side of what could have become a north-south mall, McVey Hall opened in 1928 to serve a variety of purposes: it housed classrooms, offices, the relocated cafeteria, the campus post office, the bookstore, and before long the radio arts department. Across Limestone and Upper streets the city gave to the university the site of the one-time city dump, more recently a park. There the university erected a new building for the College of Education and its model school. In 1930 the university jumped across Rose Street for the first time and located the Dairy Products Building on a small plot at the northwestern corner of the Experiment Station Farm. Dean Cooper could accept the encroachment because it was, after all, a part of his domain; nevertheless, it was a leap prophetic of things to come.

The crowning glories of the decade's building activities were Memorial Hall and a new library. The university supplemented private contributions for a war memorial and built an auditorium in New England church style with an open-air

The Margaret I. King Library, named for the university's long-time library director, was completed in 1931. For a few years, the front of the building offered an unobstructed view toward McLean Stadium and Guignol Theater.

amphitheater behind it. With its stage and pipe organ, Memorial Hall filled the long-standing need for a facility for concerts, lectures, and some activities of the music department.

The new library, central to the instructional program, greatly improved the image of the institution. The money came from a windfall under Kentucky tax law, which allocated to the university a portion of the return from the state inheritance tax: the estate of the late Mrs. Robert Bingham of Louisville paid enough in taxes that the university could afford the balance. Yet people began at once to ask how long the building would be big enough. The library's holdings were three times the 36,000 volumes at McVey's accession, and the annual rate of increase was accelerating.

All of this building resulted in the relocation of some departments and colleges, and by the time the Depression halted campus construction the university's geography seemed settled for the time being. Another spurt of enrollment, however, with the accompanying increase of new instructional needs, would force the institution to engage once again in the old game of catch-up.

To the southeast of the campus, beyond Rose Street and east of Nicholasville Pike and extending toward Tates Creek Pike, was a large area of privately owned farmland ripe for development. Residences were springing up along the pikes that bordered it. Contiguous with the existing Experiment Station Farm of 243 acres, the land attracted the attention of Dean Cooper, who saw it as the natural location for an enlarged station

farm. Hastening to head off developers, he made himself a prime mover of purchases which by 1930 enlarged the farm to almost its maximum size. Though in his later years he tried to resist threats of encroachment on his beloved farm, the times and the future of university development were against him. Out the Newtown Pike in the 1950s and 1960s , however, the university acquired about 2,500 acres of land for agriculture's future needs.

In the 1920s, the university acquired large amounts of land. In 1923 the E.O. Robinson Foundation gave to it nearly 15,000 acres of timberland in Breathitt County, and an agricultural substation with forestry operations was established at Quicksand. In the next year the generosity of the people in Caldwell County provided land for the Princeton substation. From time to time other experimental and demonstration lands were acquired throughout the state.

The university was farsighted in acquiring land for the Agricultural Experiment Station. But getting peripheral land around the campus and the money to build on it for academic purposes would be more difficult and painfully slower.

Arthur M. Miller (above left), UK's first football coach (briefly in 1892) and professor of geology, was the first dean of the College of Arts and Sciences (1907-17). He spent his entire academic career at the university in its various incarnations.

Mathematician Paul P. Boyd (above right) succeeded Miller as dean of the College of Arts and Sciences from 1917 to 1947. Before the post-World War II proliferation, the College of Arts and Sciences included the activities that garnered most campus attention, and the respected dean was correspondingly prominent.

With the early settlement of the most pressing problems, McVey turned to bringing the university into the new postwar world. He concentrated upon the renamed College of Arts and Sciences, and by the mid-1920s new departments, new faculty, and new programs had been added to the college—music, art and design, health and hygiene, psychology, political science, and a combined department of economics and sociology. Botany, zoology, and bacteriology were transferred into the college from agriculture. Military science and physical education, hitherto unattached, also became departments in the college. Home economics moved into the College of Agriculture. In 1923 the department of education became a separate college; and two years later a College of Commerce was created, with economics joined to it. These changes and expansions promised the growth of graduate studies, and to foster them the Graduate School was recreated.

Among the new, often young faculty recruited for new programs or to strengthen old ones, many remained to finish out their careers at UK, supplying much of the faculty leadership into the 1960s.

(Text continues on page 99.)

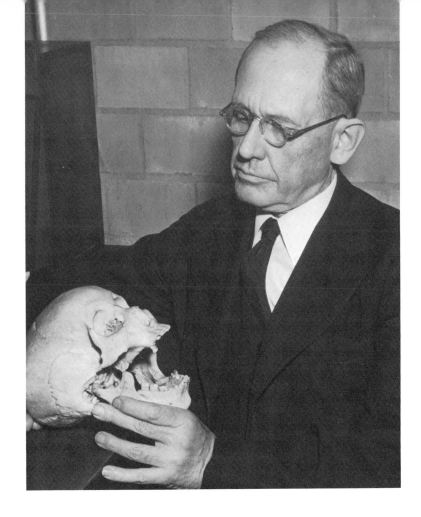

William D. Funkhouser, head of the zoology department, was one of the young men McVey brought in soon after he became president. When the Graduate School was reorganized, Funkhouser became dean in 1925 and served until his death some 20 years later. He was a publishing scholar, a popular teacher, and a faculty leader in campus affairs for nearly three decades.

I Specialize In

ALL KINDS OF ANIMALS

COME TAKE A COURSE
WITH ME

Dr. Funkhouser

Another of the young men who came to UK during the post-World War I expansion was Morris Scherago, at left. With a doctorate in veterinary medicine, he came as an instructor of bacteriology. For three decades he was a faculty leader, and the department he headed — later named microbiology — produced many doctoral graduates who became eminent in the field, especially in public health. At right is research associate Herbert H. Hall.

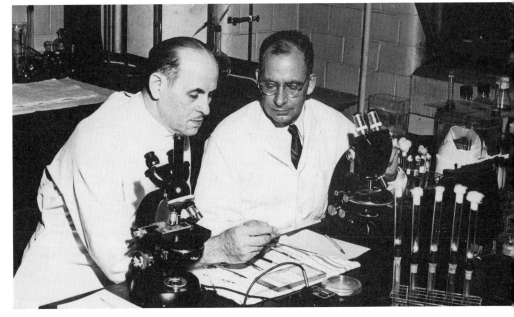

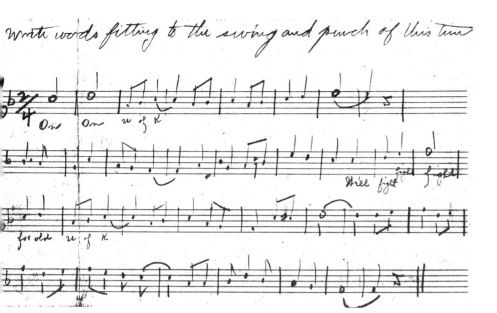

write words fitting to the swing and punch of this tune

The university had no music department until Carl A. Lampert (1874-1949) arrived in 1918 to organize and head one. Few realize when they sing "Hail! Kentucky" at commencement or "On! On! U of K" at football games that it was Lampert who penned these compositions in the mid-1920s.

J.T.C. ("Cotton") Noe, who served the university from the early years of the century until his retirement in 1934, was better known for his poetic endeavors than for his work as professor of education. The Kentucky legislature named him poet laureate of the Commonwealth in 1926. The pep song he composed in State University days never caught on.

With a doctoral degree from the University of Minnesota, William D. Valleau (far left) came to UK in 1919 as a plant pathologist and spent the rest of his scholarly career here. He attained international eminence in his field and was especially admired by Kentucky tobacco farmers for virtually saving the industry from destruction by plant disease. He died in Lexington in 1974.

After twenty years in the chemistry department, Ralph N. Maxson (near left) became head in the mid-1920s and served for almost another twenty years.

Upon his appointment in 1910, Ezra Gillis (at right) became the first true registrar at UK. He made the office a significant one and was nationally recognized for his work in the field. Following his retirement in 1937, he organized and directed the Bureau of Source Materials of Higher Education, which developed into the university archives. He remained active until his death in 1957 at the age of 91. Here, he and Allie Washington, a Lexington educator, are discussing materials relating to early black schools in Lexington.

Frank Fowler (left) became director of the Romany Theater in 1928 and the following year renamed it the Guignol. He is shown here saddened by the fire that demolished the theater in 1947. A year later Fowler moved to California. Wallace Briggs, who succeeded him, had the pleasure of seeing Guignol Theater reestablished in the new Fine Arts Building, which opened in February 1950 with "Medea."

Coming to the College of Education in 1929, Leo M. Chamberlain (above) became Registrar in 1937 and a decade later vice-president, a position he retained until his retirement some 15 years later. In his quiet way he was a respected and effective force in university affairs under Presidents Donovan and Dickey.

UK's animal husbandry department was recognized for its prize-winning sheep, an industry that flourished in Kentucky before the 1960s. Head herdsman Harold Barber, known as "Mr. Shepherd of America," was famous for his many winning entries in international livestock shows. He came to UK in 1922, several years after arriving in central Kentucky from England, and died in 1960.

Construction on McVey Hall, opposite Kastle Hall, was completed in 1928. The nearest building on this side of McVey for another few years was the Experiment Station across Washington Avenue. The university post office, after being damaged in the 1928 flood of Alumni Gym, moved to McVey, occupying basement quarters adjoining the campus bookstore. The upper floors have served various departments over the years; today the building houses the computing center and WBKY, the university radio station.

Between the wars the hill below
White Hall (left) was a botanical
garden maintained by the Lexington
Garden Club and the departments
of botany and horticulture. Other
flower gardens on campus were an
azalea garden near White Hall, a
dahlia garden near Mechanical Hall,
and the pretty little courtyard
behind Romany (later Guignol)
Theater (above). The frame building
on Euclid Avenue housed the
theater, music and art departments.

Boyd Hall, the second girls' dormitory, was built in 1925. Later dormitories have since enveloped it: Jewell Hall (1940), Keeneland Hall (1954), Holmes Hall (1958), and Blazer Hall (1960), creating a complex bounded by Limestone St., Euclid Ave., and Martin Luther King, Jr., Blvd. (formerly Harrison Avenue).

Another 1920s building was Taylor Education Building (right), named for William F. Taylor, dean of the college from 1923 until his death in 1949. It housed both the College of Education and the University School. A later extension to the rear of the left wing was the Dickey Building, opened for classes in 1964.

The UK Women's Club, comprising mainly faculty wives, gathered at a spring event in the mid-1920s. Mrs. McVey is standing, seventh from left. Faculty wives at all universities of that period were a stately lot who carried themselves with composed dignity.

Frances Jewell (later Mrs. McVey), a recent Vassar graduate and instructor in English, directed the Shakespeare Festival on May 17, 1916. The actors in the four plays were members of the English Club, as were the Elizabethan barmaids who offered tarts and ginger beer to the audience sitting on folding chairs on the lawn sloping away from Main Building. Here a Maypole dance is inserted, appropriately, into a performance of "A Midsummer Night's Dream."

The celebration of May Day gradually took new forms. By 1926 the maypole had been replaced by a May Queen, and later there was a parade. Here the Dutch theme suggested spring tulips.

Phi Sigma Kappa members gather nearly a decade later in celebration of the fraternity's arrival on campus in 1926. The 1920s saw several other national fraternities and sororities come to UK so that by the 1930s there were 17 fraternities and 9 sororities. They were at the height of their influence upon campus affairs in succeeding years until the student protest movement of the 1960s marked them as objects of hostility. But that troubled time passed and anti-Greek sentiment diminished. Now there are 22 national fraternities and 16 sororities at UK.

In the early 1920s the university band also served as the ROTC band, playing for military reviews as well as football games. Their uniforms were ROTC uniforms, including the wrap leggings, a carryover from wartime. This is the 1922-23 band, smaller than when it played at games.

Elmer Sulzer came to UK in 1926 as instructor of music. After organizing the first co-ed band (below), he turned to radio. In cooperation with WHAS in 1929, he organized the mountain listening centers to bring radio to remote areas of Eastern Kentucky. On campus he set up a radio studio in 1933, created the department of radio arts in 1941, established WBKY-FM three years later, and became the university's first publicity director. After World War II he went to Indiana University, leaving behind monuments to his memory.

"The latest in wrestling holds seen in Buell Armory," said the Kentuckian of a 1920 dance. This was the beginning of the Jazz Age. Short skirts and bell-bottomed trousers were yet to come, but bobbed hair had arrived.

The engineering students were always a close-knit and sociable group, and their annual costume ball—this one from 1921—was a long-standing event.

A tender scene from "Death Takes a Holiday," a Guignol Theater production of the 1932-33 season starring Ruth Wehle and Goodson Knight.

UK students in search of food had to find the latest location for the cafeteria. The original mess hall was abandoned in 1919 in favor of this dining area (right) in the basement of the Administration Building. A decade later the facility moved to the third floor of the new McVey Hall and remained there until the Student Union Commons opened in 1937. The increased size with each move reflected the growth in numbers of students and faculty. Food prices too increased.

One of the most celebrated visitors to the university was Eleanor Roosevelt, who lectured on campus and stayed at Maxwell Place in early July 1934. Here she is seen with the McVeys and with Governor Ruby Laffoon on the steps of the president's home.

A McVey-Maxwell Place tradition was the senior breakfast on the lawn, given by the McVeys at their own expense, for graduating students and their guests.

Augustus Lukeman's statue of James K. Patterson was dedicated in 1934 and situated in the section of the campus that Patterson knew best—

near the Administration Building, the Carnegie Library, the old dorm, and the president's home. Provided by money left by Patterson and his

brother Walter, the statue stood on this site for nearly 34 years before being moved to its present location west of the Patterson Office Tower.

In the years between 1918 and the mid-1920s, then, the university underwent unprecedented expansion, modernization, and infusion of new spirit. The Great Depression that began in 1929 affected the university's life in various ways, some of them contradictory. The low point of both income and enrollment did not come until 1934, when enrollment fell by 1,000 students to 3,822. In 1930-31, income from state appropriations was a record sum of $1,315,462, but it fell to half that three years later. In 1941-42, when enrollment reached a new record of 6,242, income from the state had recovered only to $944,000. During the Depression, as later during the war, various federal monies offset the decline

in state support; they could not, however, be counted on as steady and predictable revenues. In that respect, the university lost ground.

Two expedients when state appropriations dwindled were to reduce expenses and to halt capital construction. In the worst years, faculty and staff suffered salary cuts and deferments, while students bore an increase in fees. Vacant teaching positions were left unfilled, and all-around economies were imposed but, although some programs were crippled, there were no fatalities.

No new buildings went up until federal funds became available, notably through the Public Works Administration, but with that assistance

Built in 1937, the Student Union filled a long-felt need. The entrance to the ground floor is in the center, facing Limestone Street. It housed the Grill, student hangout of the 1940s and '50s, the Commons, and a once-controversial barber shop. Above is the Great Hall extending the entire width of the building. Additions in the 1960s and '70s extended the building and its parking lot onto the one-time football practice field.

and proceeds from bond sales, the late 1930s and early 1940s saw the university complete an impressive number of new buildings: the law building, Lafferty Hall (1936); the original part of the Student Union (1937); the engineering quadrangle (1938); a women's dormitory, Jewell Hall (1939); a central heating plant on Upper Street (1940); the controversial aeronautical research laboratory (1941); the home economics building (1942); and the biological sciences building (1942). Besides this construction on the main campus, a second addition was made to the Experiment Station building.

Some of the construction generated controversies. If there was a desire for a swimming pool in the Student Union, there was opposition to a barber shop. The law and engineering buildings added to the architectural diversity of the campus in ways displeasing to many. Though no one contested the need for a new central plant to eliminate the twenty individual boilers heating buildings around the campus, preservationists objected to demolition of the picturesque heating plant, with its ivy-covered smokestack, directly behind the administration building; the old monument was thought by some to be as romantic as a Gothic ruin. The aeronautical laboratory agitated the campus because the donor, Swedish industrialist Axel Wenner-Gren, was suspected of Nazi sympathies during World War II. Not un-

(Text continues on page 111.)

Until the mid-1960s the Student Union Grill
was the campus gathering place, and the
Commons, serving good and inexpensive
food, was the most popular eating place.
Lawrence Roberts, manager of the Grill in
its most popular days and always called
"Mr. Roberts," was one of the best known
persons on campus. While the Grill was a
busy and noisy place, students mingled better there than in any of its more recent
replacements.

Women's basketball was well established by 1920-21, when Sarah Blanding (back row) coached the Kittennettes. In 1923 she was captain and played forward, while a law student named A.B. "Happy" Chandler coached the team to a 5-3 record. Blanding was later dean of women at UK and president of Vassar. One of the dorm towers is named for her.

The choice of mascot for the university's teams is supposed to have been inspired by a description of an early football team that "fought like wildcats." The Kentuckian followed with an essay on the admirable qualities of the wildcat as the symbol of team spirit. After that, it was a natural transition to the presence of a real wildcat at football games. The first one appeared in 1921.

Spirits were high among UK students as they formed a living "K" on Stoll Field before the 1920 game with Centre. Spirits were low as shadows lengthened: Centre won 49-0.

John Mauer was Wildcat basketball coach from the fall of 1927 through spring 1930. He is credited with introducing the "UK system." Here he sits with his last UK team: left to right, front row: manager Leonard Weakley, Stanley Milward, Cecil Combs, Paul McBrayer, Lawrence "Big" McGinnis, and Carey Spicer. Middle row: Mauer, Jake Bronston, Ercel Little, Bill Trott, and George Yates. Back row: Hays Owens, Larry Crump, Milton Cavana, Bill Kleiser, and Louis "Little" McGinnis.

In the early years, many UK students participated in sports. Here are the wrestling team of 1922 (right) and the rifle team of 1922-23 (below). Student photographer F.A.C. Thompson (to whom we owe a number of pictures) is third from left in the front row of the rifle team. The K-Club, composed of letter winners, and SUKY, the student pep organization, also existed this early.

John "Shipwreck" Kelly (left), nicknamed for a flagpole sitter who performed atop the Lafayette Hotel, performed numerous feats of his own on the UK gridiron from 1928 through 1932. He went on to play pro football for the Brooklyn Dodgers and later became co-owner of the team. Ralph Kercheval (below), another UK football star, 1932-34, also played for the Dodgers through the 1939 season, winning renown as a punter and placekicker.

Captain of the 1925 UK football team and All-Conference back, Albert D. (Ab) Kirwan (above) returned to UK as head football coach from 1938 to 1944. In a remarkable career, he was later dean of men, professor of history, and finally president of the university from 1968 to 1970.

Whether shouting at an official or at one of his players, Adolph Rupp, the 'man in the brown suit,' had fire in his eyes and sarcasm on his tongue. Assistant Coach Harry Lancaster appears somewhat calmer in the 1958 game in Memorial Coliseum shown above. Rupp came to Kentucky in 1930 out of high school basketball in Illinois and coached until he had to accept retirement in 1972. During the intervening years he won greater fame for more reasons than any other college basketball coach. He is remembered as much for his flamboyant personality as for the achievements of his teams. Though only the latter go down in the record books, UK and Kentucky history and mythology will long preserve the memory of the Baron of Basketball. It revives and is told anew with each new basketball season.

James Lowry Cogar (B.A. 1927) was one of two UK alumni responsible for the restoration of Shakertown at Pleasant Hill. Earl D. Wallace (B.S. 1921) was the other. They came together after making distinguished careers, Wallace as a petroleum industry executive and investment manager, Cogar—after architectural studies at Harvard and Yale—in numerous restoration projects, notably at Colonial Williamsburg, where he was for a time curator. Wallace was the driving force behind the organization and funding efforts for Shakertown; Cogar was concerned with the actual restoration work. The restored Shaker village stands as their monument. Cogar died in 1987.

The annual dinner of the Chicago Alumni Association was held at the Great Northern Hotel, March 27, 1918. The attendance of 70 was large considering that the university had by then granted only about 2,000 degrees to persons scattered to all points of the compass, including war service.

Unique among UK alumni, P.J. Conkwright (B.A. 1928) became one of the best known book designers in the publishing field.

Only a year after his 1924 gradua-tion from UK, John Thomas Scopes became nationally known as the science teacher found guilty of violating the Tennessee anti-evolution law. The trial was the center of national attention in 1925 partly because the rival attorneys were Clarence Darrow for the defense and William Jennings Bryan for the prosecution. During Scopes's undergraduate days at UK, President McVey was leading the fight against attempts to enact a similar anti-evolution law in Kentucky, a fact that may have aroused Scopes against the Tennessee law, which was not repealed until 1967.

Paul Porter (Ll.B. 1929) went to Washington to become a well known member of the New Deal administration and then a partner in a leading Washington law firm, where he remained promi-nent for some thirty years. He died in 1975.

In 1929, James A. Yates of Ottawa, Kansas, received the first earned doctoral degree awarded by the university, in the field of education. State College conferred the B.A. degree upon him in 1890 and State University the M.A. in 1909. Yates was the only person to receive earned degrees under each of the school's three names.

Virginia Clay McClure (B.A. 1912, M.A. 1928, Ph.D. 1934) was the first woman to earn a doctoral degree at UK. Her history dissertation, "The Settlement of the Kentucky Appalachian Highlands," was a generation ahead of the crowd in demonstrating the opportunities for scholarly work on Appalachia. McClure taught history at Lexington's Henry Clay High School for 25 years before her retirement in 1959.

The late John F. Day (B.A. 1935) went into radio and print journalism; he was vice-president of CBS news and a European correspondent of Time-Life magazines before retiring to a more tranquil career as publisher and editor of the Exmouth Journal in Devon, England.

Joe Creason (B.A. 1940), folksy columnist of the Louisville Courier-Journal and president of the Alumni Association in 1969-70, was one of the best-loved newspaper personalities in Kentucky. The Creason Lectures, begun in 1978 and sponsored by the journalism department, bring to the campus each year some outstanding figure in the field of journalism. Creason died in 1974.

Elizabeth Hardwick (B.A. 1938, M.A. 1939) made a literary career in New York, particularly as a drama critic and as a founder, with her husband, Robert Lowell, of the New York Review of Books.

With president Herman Donovan standing before the portrait of his predecessor, this picture symbolizes the aura that McVey cast over his two successors and, in a sense, over the Board as long as it met in the Administration Building.

til 1945 did a masterful report by Dean of the University Leo Chamberlain refute allegations that had grown out of wartime hysteria.

On July 1, 1940, President McVey retired, leaving behind a magnificent reputation for fairness, integrity, dignity, and understanding of the proper role of a university president. His successor would face the formidable burden of trying to maintain the advances the university had made while laboring under the shadow of affectionate memories of President McVey and his late wife. The awareness of being judged against McVey's example might be uncomfortable.

Dean Cooper served as acting president while a search committee sought for a successor for McVey. Not until April 1, 1941, was it ready to make a recommendation to the board, and on that day strange things happened. The board went into executive session from which the acting president, who had not permitted himself to be a candidate, was excluded. The trustees then rewrote McVey's constitution of the university. They created an enormously powerful department of business management and control, and named Frank Peterson, a state financial official, as comptroller. Without mentioning the university's Faculty Senate by name, the board replaced it with a body to be called the University Faculty—composed entirely of administrators.

When graduates did not number in the thousands, presidents actually signed diplomas. Here is Donovan bending to the task.

Popular as McVey had been among the faculty and the general public, there had clearly been a concealed opposition to some of his work.

Never before had the faculty been so completely excluded from university affairs. At its last meeting of the school year, the old senate asked for reconsideration of the action abolishing it, as did the *Kentucky Kernel* and the Student Government Association on June 4. That was all, except for bitter memories, a decline of the university's prestige, and a burdensome heritage to hand over to the new president.

The board at this same meeting went on to elect the new president to whom this package of changes would be delivered. Governor Keen Johnson, the presiding officer, left the room to call Herman L. Donovan, president of Eastern State Teachers' College, and obtain his acceptance of the invitation.

Unlike his predecessor, Donovan lacked national stature either in his professional field, education, or as president of one of four teachers colleges in an educationally backward state. The circumstances of the appointment and reasonable suspicions of political influence behind it dimmed whatever luster he might have brought to the presidency. The future of the university at that moment seemed as inauspicious as some had feared at Barker's appointment in 1910.

Donovan wrote some years afterward that had he known of the board's abolition of the Faculty Senate, he would have declined the offer of the presidency. Incredible as it seems, he learned of the action, he said, only on his first day on the job three months later; the board never officially informed him of it. He considered it his "first task" to persuade the trustees to rectify their action. It took him two years to argue them into replacing their "University Faculty" with a new body of the same name but with faculty members

Herman Donovan and his wife, Nell, stand in the front entranceway of Maxwell Place.

making up a majority. Donovan thought his hard-won success "one of the outstanding accomplishments of my years as President of the University." This point needs emphasis because it reveals Donovan at his fighting best. His victory restored the faculty's self-respect and showed Donovan as a champion of faculty rights, privileges, and dignity as they were understood at the time.

The title of his book *Keeping the University Free and Growing* (1959) reflects Donovan's continual struggle to do just that. In the early 1920s

During World War II there was a military presence at UK, but ASTP members' academic work while awaiting assignment to military units attracted less attention from photographers than had World War I activities.

freedom of teaching was at stake in the controversy emerging in many states over the teaching of evolution. President McVey led the defense of academic freedom in Kentucky and won a close victory in the General Assembly. The 1925 Scopes trial in Tennessee, a continuation of the same conflict, had an unusual interest for Kentucky. Not only was John T. Scopes a UK alumnus, but victorious anti-evolution forces hoped to revive the attack in Frankfort. As it happened, two anti-evolution bills died in the 1926 legislature.

As the new president of UK, Donovan had to be constantly on guard against threats from outside the school. A sectarian request for a Bible course to be taught from a denominational point of view was dropped when Donovan quietly cited the attorney general's opinion that the state constitution forbade such a course. As Donovan said, "To yield to all the demands that are made upon [the president] in a single year would wreck the institution."

While normally he tried to stifle such intrusions by working quietly, in 1950 he went public against a horrifying assault from Frankfort. A new law gave to the Division of Personnel in the state's Department of Finance the authority to fix compensation schedules for university and state college employees. Unable to sway the state senate or the governor prior to the passage of the act, Donovan mobilized powerful state, regional, and national educational forces and public opinion against this blatant attempt to politicize higher education. The pressure on Frankfort overwhelmed the politicians, and in 1952 the legislature and the new governor, Lawrence Wetherby, corrected the law, returning to the governing boards of the institutions their hitherto uncontested authority to determine salaries for their faculties and staffs. Donovan's victory rescued higher education in Kentucky not only from humiliation but from the threat of censure from na-

tional accrediting bodies. In fighting to keep the university free, Donovan served both the school and the state better than people had expected.

The Second World War's impact on the campus was much like that of the first because at the outset the government turned to the nation's schools for assistance. The first students to feel the effects of the war were the 1,175 enrolled in the ROTC. Within a few months nearly all of

The Guignol fire of January 1947 left the music department homeless, but by April it had set up shop in these quonset huts located in front of the Student Union. They were among many temporary facilities of the period, most of them necessitated by the postwar influx of students.

In September 1946, at the south-west corner of the farm, prospective tenants helped out as army surplus barracks went up in a hurry to create Shawneetown. This temporary student housing was replaced by a permanent apartment complex in 1957.

them were in service. From then until the end of the war the male portion of the student body was drastically diminished, and women played a proportionately larger role in campus activities than ever before. The *Kentuckian* said in 1944 that "it was a woman's world on the *Kentucky Kernel* this year," and the staff of the yearbook was almost entirely feminine. The university had no football season in 1943, and of the twelve schools in the Southeastern Conference only four played regular schedules.

As in World War I the university carried out training programs for the army. Almost 3,100 soldiers went through the Engineer Specialist School up to September 1943, by which time the Army Specialized Training Program (ASTP) was offering college work for recruits awaiting assignment to regular army units. About 3,000 soldiers went through that program at UK. The men in both programs were housed in the Phoenix Hotel and in university dormitories and were taught by university faculty, some hastily recruited for the purpose. Many younger members of the faculty entered various kinds of government service, so there was no lack of work for those who remained at home. Of the UK men and women who went into service—7,644 students, alumni, and faculty—334 gave their lives. Their names are inscribed in Memorial Coliseum, the monument erected to commemorate them.

The Social Sciences building, better known to students and faculty as Splinter Hall, was remodeled in 1947 from army surplus barracks. It hardly improved the view from the front of King Library. It burned to the ground in 1968, leaving a space eventually filled by Margaret I. King Library North.

Learning from the previous war, the university expected an influx of veterans when peace returned. This prospect was certain after June 1944, when the federal GI Bill provided financial aid to returnees and veterans enrolling for the first time. In 1944-45, enrollment fell to the wartime low of 3,156. With the return of peace the next year, it doubled.

If the sudden increase was expected, its size was not. Many of the veterans were married, and many of these had small children, but housing in Lexington was virtually unobtainable. With government surplus prefabs available for little cost except transportation and erection, the university by 1947 had built two villages for mar-

ried veterans and new faculty, Cooperstown and Shawneetown, at opposite corners of the Experiment Station Farm. On the campus proper, temporary classrooms dotted the academic landscape. Perhaps the best (or worst) remembered was the social science building in front of the scenic entrance to King Library. Occupants called it Splinter Hall; as the years passed, they feared it might become permanent. It did in fact remain in use for twenty years.

Postwar enrollment peaked at 10,169 in 1950, by which time most of the veterans had passed through the university. A drop followed, and then a normal pattern of growth set in. New construction was already under way. In quick succession

The first postwar permanent classroom-office building, completed in 1950, brought music, art, and theater together again after the three-year separation caused by the Guignol fire of 1947. The Fine Arts Building stands on what was once the site of Mulligan's Spring. The McLean Stadium press box can be seen to the left of the theater tower.

around 1950, several buildings were completed: Bowman Hall, the fourth men's dorm, to enclose the quadrangle; the Animal Pathology Building; the first permanent postwar classroom-office building, Fine Arts; the Service Building across Limestone Street; and the Grehan Journalism Building in the midcampus mall extending toward the biological sciences building.

The most ambitious and costly projects were along Euclid Avenue, where the impatient public watched the progress of a basketball palace and the enlargement of McLean Stadium to a seating capacity of about 35,000, double its previous size. Under a new coach, Paul Bryant, football prospects excited the fans, and basketball was by

this time the glory of the university and its constituency; the demand for seats in Alumni Gym far exceeded the supply.

The basketball team had not suffered a losing season since 1927, and by the end of the war Adolph Rupp's teams had compiled a phenomenal record in and out of the Southeastern Conference. The war had postponed construction of a fieldhouse, and by the time the first two postwar legislatures appropriated funds for it, the plans had changed. President Donovan insisted on a general-purpose auditorium building that not only would seat about 11,000 for basketball but could be used for other university gatherings as well. A swimming pool and offices for the

The newly completed Memorial Coliseum as seen from atop the football stadium. The near segment houses the swimming pool, the auditorium-basketball arena is in the center, and the athletic department offices occupy the far section. The 1951 commencement was the first held in the Coliseum. No longer was there reason to worry about bad weather or a shortage of seats.

The Enoch Grehan Journalism Building (below), built in 1951, for the first time gave the journalism department and the Kernel *their own home.*

When Frazee Hall caught fire in January 1956, arson was suspected but never proved. The fire began in the men's restroom in the basement and roared up the stairwell. On learning of the fire, the first reaction of at least one professor was, "My manuscript is in my office!" The interior was restored much as it had been.

athletic department were also included in the plans. After the cornerstone was laid in 1949, the building was dedicated as a war memorial to be called Memorial Coliseum.

The most grandiose project in the university's history up to that time, the Coliseum cost about $4 million, of which the legislature provided 75 percent. The newly formed Athletic Association made itself liable for the bonds sold to pay the remainder, expecting to retire them from athletic revenues. That is, bondholders had a stake and the association a sense of urgency in the success of UK football and basketball. Donovan had already come to believe in a correlation between winning teams and legislative generosity toward the university. Although he liked to talk about the auditorium function of the Coliseum, the public knew it as "the house that Rupp built."

In the first years after the war, the university made notable advances on three academic fronts. In 1945 it incorporated the Kentucky Research Foundation to solicit and administer gifts and grants from individuals, foundations, corporate bodies, and government. With the phenomenal growth of government spending on research through such agencies as the National Science Foundation, solicitation of funds for the support of research and various projects within the university became a major enterprise. The Research Foundation came into being none too early and grew into a major organ of the institution, though it functions—like the scholars who conduct research—without receiving much attention outside the university.

The shackles that bound university personnel to the $5,000 salary limitation for state officials—imposed by the 1891 state constitution and affirmed by a 1942 Court of Appeals decision—were finally broken by a test case in 1947, and just in time: the restriction was beginning to pinch hard and threaten the very existence of the university.

In the new postwar world another problem was clamoring for the attention of the University of Kentucky and many others as well. The state's Day Law of 1904 prohibited the teaching of blacks and whites in the same school at all levels. Earlier attempts to challenge the law had not been pushed to decision, but in 1948 Lyman Johnson sued in Federal District Court in Lexington after being denied admission to the UK Graduate School. Though the decision did not

The original Cooperstown was hastily erected immediately after the war at the northern limit of the Experiment Station farm as housing for the influx of married students, but was replaced within a decade by these solid and attractive structures.

Lyman Johnson, right, with R.B. Atwood, president of Kentucky State College, emerges from Federal District Court in Lexington in the glow of victory following his suit to gain admission to UK in March 1949. This picture is all the more dramatic for the dignified bearing of the two. It was an important victory. Blacks were admitted to graduate and professional programs at UK beginning with the summer session of 1949, as seen in the registration scene below, and to the undergraduate program from 1954 on.

overturn the Day Law, Judge H. Church Ford directed the university to admit Johnson because Kentucky State College—a school for blacks in Frankfort—did not provide professional or graduate education.

Assured of the court's protection, the university not only admitted Johnson but enrolled other blacks as well in the summer school of 1949. Students and faculty for the most part welcomed this new order. Without fuss or incident the university continued to enroll blacks pending a decision on the constitutionality of the Day Law.

Instances of cross burnings at the front of the campus by undiscovered persons were not taken to reflect student, faculty, or community opinion and did not mar the good order that prevailed before and after the court proceedings. Throughout, the university community and the citizens of Lexington, blacks and whites alike, behaved superbly. The board of trustees, after strenuous discussion, accepted President Donovan's recommendation not to appeal Judge Ford's decision. In 1954 the United States Supreme Court in *Brown* v. *Board of Education* settled the constitutional question for Kentucky and the nation. By that time the university had put behind it much that would have kept it from becoming great.

Until the early 1960s the University of Kentucky was predominantly an undergraduate institution. It did not award a doctoral degree until 1929, and the annual number of graduate degrees increased only slowly during the next thirty years. In 1920 graduate degrees were only 5 percent of the total awarded; by 1960 the

The present system of advanced registration is hailed as less painful than the crowded registrations of an earlier era, first in Alumni Gym and later (as here) in the Coliseum.

Panty raids were a nationwide campus rage in the early 1950s. The girls at the window don't seem alarmed.

The pushcart derby was part of the changing format of the Little Kentucky Derby, the annual celebration of spring. Athletics Director Bernie Shively is the starter here as contestants take to Limestone Street.

The quarterback and the cheerleader—Bob Hardy and Joanne Shelton—pose on the wall in front of Barker Hall in the mid-1950s, epitomizing the clean-cut look of the bobby socks era.

number had increased to 20 percent, with 33 of the 347 graduate degrees in that year being doctorates.

Though the composition of the student body was changing statistically, campus life retained its traditional undergraduate character. The intimacy and homogeneity of earlier times remained evident even though the total enrollment of the Lexington campus by 1960 had grown to 7,285 with a larger proportion of graduate students than formerly. They were less visible about the campus, however, being tucked away in libraries or laboratories.

The graduates of that year passed through a university greatly different from the one the class of 1920 entered. World War I and the early postwar years had brought about changes in the world outside that affected programs and life within the university. The return to what was called normalcy did not bring back prewar nor-

malcy, for it included the Jazz Age, the prosperity of the 1920s, and the dawning of the age of radio and automobiles within reach of ordinary persons. College generations of the years 1928-36 lived with the Great Depression, the New Deal, and continued hard times. The succeeding generation was in school during the world's descent toward war and later helped fight it.

During the buoyant 1920s and the depressed 1930s, students displayed a sense of humor missing among later generations of students. Humor magazines existed on many university campuses for longer or shorter periods of time; nationally, *College Humor*, with its flappers and sheiks, was popular. Students at UK, mostly journalism majors, made three attempts at humor magazines before World War II: the *Kampus Kat*, *Sour Mash*, and the *Wildcat*. Students of more recent decades would consider them about as titillating as the tales of Peter Rabbit.

Sadie Hawkins Day, sponsored by Keys, was a campus event of the 1950s, when Al Capp's comic strip about life in Dogpatch was popular. On that day men were fair game for relentless pursuing females. A dance in the Student Center was the official ending of the day. Jane Webb and Tony Rotunno were considered 1950's "best-looking Dog-patchers."

In the student body of the first years after World War II, many of the veterans pressing to make up for lost time were a bit older than earlier undergraduates, and they took their college work very seriously as they prepared to go out into the better world they had fought for. Then, until about 1960, students were surrounded though not overwhelmed by the Cold War and international tensions; still, they found college more tranquil than had any others since 1916. Times were good; the cost of living was not out of hand; automobiles were plentiful even if parking spaces were becoming less so. The winning tradition of basketball continued year after year, almost predictably; football after the war was doing better than it had for a long time and even knew years of glory, especially in 1950-51; intramural sports were prominent, and rivalries were keen. The Student Union, completed just before the war, offered the first spacious ballroom the campus had ever known, available in time to bid farewell to the waltz and welcome jitterbugging; the Student Union commons served the best cafeteria food that students at UK had ever enjoyed on campus, and at reasonable prices; and a cozy grill adjoined it as a social center presided over by "Mr. Roberts." Its like had not been known before, and there has been nothing quite like it since the 1950s.

The campus was noticeably free of tensions among students and between them and the faculty and administration; such as existed were handled quietly behind the scenes and did not disturb the peace of the campus. Student militancy was not in vogue, and students had not learned how to publicize their concerns. The important Lyman Johnson case did not ruffle the even tenor of campus life, even though it was well known among members of the university community. Campus disturbances, such as panty raids, had no political or ideological content. The raids might call up some rowdiness, but they were conducted in good spirit, were quickly dispersed, and did not portend social unrest.

If students were not uptight about the state of society, neither were they apathetic toward life and learning. But with the shadows of two world wars and then the Korean conflict not yet behind them, most welcomed a respite from military and civil conflict.

After World War II, bobby-soxers and their male contemporaries appeared as the children of the Roaring Twenties' flaming youth. In spirit there was little difference between the Model Ts of the 1920s or the rumble seats and open Packard convertibles cruising Limestone Street in the 1930s, and the automobile fins of the 1950s and 1960s pulling into Jerry's. The short-skirted, silk-stockinged flappers and the bell- bottomed sheiks of the Jazz Age, the more sober-hued

students of the Depression era, and the bobby soxers and their boyfriends in loafers or saddle shoes and slacks and sweaters were on the whole an attractive lot, neat, well-mannered, and lively. The word "boring" was not a staple of their vocabularies. Prohibition—and in 1933 its repeal—created some problems on campus, and cigarettes were thought to bespeak social sophistication, but hard drugs were not part of the college scene until the 1960s, when humor departed from the nation's campuses.

When Kentucky played Purdue to open Memorial Coliseum in December 1950, UK basketball stood higher in public esteem than ever before. During construction of the Coliseum, UK won the National Collegiate Athletic Association (NCAA) championship in 1948 and again in

George Blanda was a solid if unexciting player on Bear Bryant's earliest UK football teams (1946-48) but came into his own when he entered professional football in 1949, beginning a career as a quarterback and an all-time scoring leader, primarily as a place kicker. His career lasted through 1975. He is the only UK player elected to the Pro Football Hall of Fame.

1949. The Fabulous Five of 1948 formed part of the U.S. Olympic team that won the championship in London. The team that opened the Coliseum won the NCAA title for the third time for the university.

The story of football does not tell of unbroken successes in the period between the wars. But in the decade following the war UK football reached unprecedented heights.

In 1945 the university formed a separately incorporated Athletic Association to control intercollegiate athletic programs through a board of directors presided over by the president. With that arrangement prevailing, no university president could be aloof from athletics. He and five appointed faculty members plus the president of the Student Government Association constituted a majority of the eleven-member board. Intercollegiate athletics were expected to be self-supporting and able to amortize bond issues for capital construction.

The Athletic Association, free of the constitutional limitation on salaries of public officials, was able to hire Paul Bryant, coach for the

LEFT: *Ralph Beard scores against Tennessee in the year of the Fabulous Five, 1947-48.*

RIGHT: *The Fabulous Five—the team unique in intercollegiate basketball history that won the NCAA championship in 1948, performed victoriously as a unit within the American squad in the 1948 Olympics (coached by Adolph Rupp), and went into pro basketball together as the Indianapolis Olympians. Team members were Ralph Beard (12), Kenny Rollins (26), Wallace "Wah Wah" Jones (27), Alex Groza (15), and Cliff Barker (23).*

OPPOSITE: *The size of this crowd justifies the postwar expansion of McLean Stadium. Half of them could not have seen the game without the enlargement of 1949.*

Coach Paul "Bear" Bryant and his two UK College Hall of Famers, Bob Gain (right), and Vito Parilli (left). Gain won the 1950 Outland Award for the nation's outstanding lineman and had a long pro career with the Cleveland Browns in the 1950s. Parilli, a favorite with UK fans, who called him the "Kentucky Babe," went on to a pro career as a player and coach. Bryant left Kentucky after the 1953 season, stopped off at Texas A&M, and then went home to Alabama to build a spectacular career.

University of Maryland. Change came swiftly: whereas the football team had gone 2-8 in 1945, in Bryant's first season (1946), the record was 7-3. Then followed seasons of 8-3, 5-3-2, and 9-3, including a loss in the Orange Bowl. The season of 1950 was the most outstanding: in the Sugar Bowl on January 1, 1951, Kentucky beat Oklahoma, generally regarded as national champion, and ended the season 11-1.

The years 1950 and 1951 were the years of glory in university athletic history. The baseball team wound up its banner 1950 season by winning the conference eastern division championship, and the football and basketball teams continued the successes into the following year. To commemorate the Sugar Bowl victory and the NCAA championship and the seasons that preceded them, Euclid Avenue between Limestone and Rose streets, passing between the Coliseum and McLean Stadium, was officially renamed the Avenue of Champions. The name never really "took" but still appears on street signs.

From a pinnacle of intercollegiate athletic fame, the fans looked forward to the year 1951-52. Then, on October 21, they learned that the university and its basketball program were in serious trouble. After things were sorted out, six players from the 1948-50 teams faced charges of accepting bribes, not to throw games but to control the scores to frustrate oddsmakers' point spreads. Five pleaded guilty and received suspended sentences; the sixth, who pleaded not guilty, submitted to a trial that resulted in a hung jury.

The NCAA barred the university from playing intercollegiate basketball during 1952-53, and President Donovan called the bribe scandal "the greatest humiliation we have ever experienced." After its year of enforced rest, however, the basketball team was undefeated in the 1953-54 season but declined the invitation to play in the

Before the 1950 season began, the Southeastern Conference coaches picked the Wildcats as the team to beat for the SEC title. The team was perhaps the best UK ever produced and went on to win the Sugar Bowl of 1951, beating national champion Oklahoma.

Here are the cheerleaders who welcomed the first of Bear Bryant's football teams in 1946. Still in the future were pom-pom girls and flagwavers.

After the 1950-51 year of athletic glories, Euclid Avenue between Rose and Limestone Streets, the section running between the Coliseum and McLean Stadium, was officially renamed Avenue of Champions. The name somehow did not take, even before basketball moved away to Rupp Arena and football moved to Commonwealth Stadium. Yet it still appears on the 1987 campus map and on street signs.

The baseball team of 1950 was SEC eastern division champion, joining the football and basketball teams in making 1950-51 perhaps the most notable year of intercollegiate athletics in the history of the university. Here outfielder Ben Zaranka takes a hefty swing.

NCAA tournaments because three players who had graduated in the off year were in graduate school and thus ineligible to play in the tournaments. The football team went 8-4 in the 1951 season, with a victory in the 1952 Cotton Bowl. After the 1953 football season, Coach Bryant left for Texas A&M, but under Blanton Collier the team continued its winning ways through the remainder of Donovan's administration, beating Tennessee in both years.

For twenty more years football and basketball continued along the Avenue of Champions before moving to Commonwealth Stadium and Rupp Arena, where the teams now play before crowds twice as large as ever before. After his retirement, Donovan said that early in his presidency, taking note of legislators' interest, he realized the necessity for achieving athletic success in order "to enlist the support of the majority of our citizens for our educational program. The policy paid off." Donovan's contention has been much debated.

After the basketball scandals, the 1953-54 teams went through the season undefeated and won the SEC championship in a playoff with LSU. The mainstays were Lou Tsioropoulos (16), Frank Ramsey (30), and Cliff Hagan (6), seen here with Coach Rupp and Assistant Coach Harry Lancaster.

Many university graduates in these years went on to successful careers, some winning renown. After World War I, graduates were able to enter into a larger variety of callings than ever before because technological innovations and social changes had created new kinds of career opportunities and because the university afforded greater opportunities for specialized education.

Between 1920 and 1955 seven students won the prized honor of Rhodes Scholarships, which, after their study at Oxford, would open doors to them in whatever careers they might choose to follow. A few alumni won prizes of international distinction. Two (one a State College graduate)

Jean Ritchie (above right, B.A. and Phi Beta Kappa 1946) quickly won international recognition as a folk and ballad singer and dulcimer player. A native of Viper, Kentucky, she has perfected these arts learned during her childhood in the mountains.

Mountain lawyer, legislator, professor of history at UK, Harry Caudill (above, Ll.B. 1948) became nationally known for his writings on Appalachia and later returned to teach history at his alma mater.

won Nobel Prizes and two received Pulitzer Prizes.

Two fields, neither one strictly new, were greatly expanded during this period: communications and sports. With the electronic revolution, communications came to embrace—besides print journalism—radio, television, publishing generally, and public relations. The enormous expansion of athletics in schools and colleges and outside them created many opportunities in coaching and sports administration. Professional sports, aided by electronics, became a major industry. Many college athletes looked upon their playing experience as preparation for involvement in sports in an academic environment or for professional careers. In the process, an intimate rela-

Bruce Denbo, left, director of the University of Kentucky Press, founded in 1943, and history department chairman Thomas D. Clark, instrumental in founding the press, examine a new book as author Carl B. Cone (center) looks on.

tionship developed between high school and college athletics, and between the latter and professional sports. Athletic programs in the university and in higher education generally no longer pretended to serve students' recreational needs alone. Like academic and professional programs, they prepared talented undergraduates for careers and thus acquired a more decided legitimacy in higher education.

The tranquillity of the campus between 1920 and 1960 may have been misleading. In offices and laboratories and libraries, creative work was going on, and a quiet kind of intellectual excite-

ment could be found. Often the university community's scholarly work attracted notice more prominently in the academic world at large than among people of the state. The installation in 1921 of a chapter of Sigma Xi, the national science honorary, was followed in 1925 by the grant of a charter from the national honorary, Phi Beta Kappa. These were not empty honors; applications for both had been turned down a few years earlier.

In 1952 the university library, with holdings of 558,442 volumes, was admitted to the select group called the Association of Research Libraries. Membership conferred recognition of the growth of the library since opening of the new building in 1931. During Donovan's administra-

Margaret I. King, UK's first librarian, looks over the collected letters written to her at the time of her retirement in 1948. She and the discipline she maintained in the Carnegie Library prompted many jokes, but they were jokes signaling respect and admiration.

tion the library filled to comfortable capacity, the collection doubling and the budget quadrupling. In the 1940s the library established the department of Special Collections, which emphasizes both Kentuckiana and archives concentrating on university materials. The department also began systematically collecting manuscripts relating particularly to Kentucky. By the 1950s, forty years after Patterson had prematurely used the phrase, the library could fairly be called a research library befitting an ambitious state university.

Closely related to these efforts was the founding in 1943 of the University of Kentucky Press, which obtained its first full-time director, Bruce Denbo, in 1950. Its production of scholarly books, many of them written by faculty members, stead-

ily increased, and the reputation of the press and the university grew together in scholarly circles. Faculty pressures provided much of the push for the library and the press, the most forceful coming from Thomas D. Clark, who became head of the history department in 1944.

The founding of the Northern Extension Center in Covington in 1948 appears more significant now than it did at the time because it can be seen as the beginning of the Community College System created by law in 1962. As the school became a center for resident instruction with a small full-time faculty, it was easy to foresee that Northern would not remain the only center where the University of Kentucky would bring academic and technical study to the people of the state in their own communities. In the name of reaching out, this function recalled the beginnings of the Agricultural Extension Service established some thirty-five years earlier.

Before Donovan retired, an old dream began to become reality: in the early 1950s the idea of offering medical education gained momentum. Opinions pro and con formed, and even among those who wanted to move forward there were differences about the scale and size of such an undertaking. In 1954 the Board of Trustees established a medical school on paper. Candidates in the gubernatorial campaign of 1955 pledged to work for it, and in 1956 the winner, A.B. Chandler, obtained $5 million from the legislature to begin construction. The board then created colleges of dentistry and nursing and established the office of vice-president of the projected Medical Center. Simultaneously, the College of Pharmacy in Louisville, which had been adopted by UK in 1947, planned to move to Lexington as soon as a building could be completed.

In April 1956 Donovan announced his intention to resign on September 1, one year before reaching the mandatory retirement age of seventy. Explaining his decision, he emphasized the arduous nature of the presidency and the need for a younger, more vigorous man to take on the task of establishing the medical school. As he prepared to leave office, excitement over the medical school caused people to overlook some of Donovan's important but less publicized achievements, such as the establishment of the University of Kentucky Press (subsequently, as scholarly publisher for the Commonwealth, renamed the University Press of Kentucky) and the Research Foundation, and his comparative generosity to the library—matters that had enhanced the reputation of the university in the academic world.

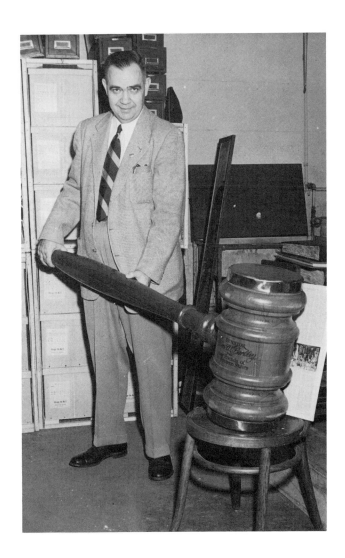

Among important gifts to the library was the collection of papers and political memorabilia of Senator/Vice President Alben Barkley, displayed here by history professor Bennett Wall, who diligently pursued the collection.

The day of reckoning—a final exam in progress in the school year 1949-50.

In every college athletic structure, some individual can be found who becomes a traditional part of it and along the way performs a variety of functions. Such was Stanley A. "Daddy" Boles. With a master's degree in English from Vanderbilt, he came to UK in 1916 to assist in physical education and intercollegiate athletics—a fact that says something about the immature state of both programs at that time. He coached the football team in 1917 and the basketball team in 1918, then became director of physical education until 1929, director of athletics until 1934, ticket manager until 1946, and manager of veterans' housing until he retired in 1955. In 1918 he started the state boys' basketball tournament and directed it for the 18 years it was held on the UK campus. He led in getting lights for Stoll Field. His paternal role toward athletes reportedly earned him his nickname. He died in 1961, age 74.

Chapter 5

The University of Kentucky
1 9 5 6 - 1 9 8 9

Previous page: The Centennial Medal marked the university's hundredth birthday. The front showed the university's founder, John B. Bowman, and first president, James K. Patterson. The obverse placed a stylized "UK" against a field of stars with the motto "Sic itur ad astra" (Thus one reaches the stars).

Named for the first dean of the college, Paul Anderson, the engineering tower (1966) expanded the engineering complex; it connects with the engineering quadrangle and with what remains of Mechanical Hall. The Robotics Center, under construction in 1989, will extend the complex to the south.

From the list presented in June 1956 by the joint faculty-board search committee, the trustees selected as the university's fifth president Frank G. Dickey, dean of the College of Education. Since the appointment came before Donovan left office, the two men cooperated in the crucial appointment of William R. Willard of Syracuse University as vice-president of the Medical Center.

Dickey became president at the age of thirty-nine, the second youngest (after James K. Patterson) in the university's history. A graduate of Transylvania, he received his doctorate in education in 1947, joined the UK faculty at once, and within two years became professor, acting dean, and dean of the College of Education. Some people wondered about two successive presidents with education backgrounds. Dickey faced the herculean task of building the medical school in addition to operating the university.

Dickey began with a biennial budget of $21 million and an enrollment of 7,170. In the academic year 1956-57 the university awarded 1,394 degrees, of which 335 were graduate degrees, including 20 doctorates. The full-time faculty of all ranks numbered about 600, with 60 percent in the College of Arts and Sciences.

One feature of the era opening in 1956 was the sheer physical growth of the university. The next few years saw monumental achievements asso-

Frank G. Dickey, named as the university's fifth president in 1956, and trustee Ralph Angelucci. To Dickey fell the task of bringing the newly established Medical Center to fruition.

This 1960 aerial photo shows the Medical Center under construction and the Experiment Station Farm as it began to be cut up for other university purposes. The men's dorm quadrangle is at bottom center and Cooperstown at left center. Cooper Drive, when cut through, will extend left to right across the middle of the picture. Commonwealth Stadium will eventually replace the clump of trees just above the center.

ciated with the new Medical Center. The dignitaries assembled in December 1957 at the northwest corner of the Experiment Station Farm along Rose Street to break ground. The Medical Sciences Building was completed in two years, and in 1960 the Colleges of Medicine and Nursing enrolled their first students. The College of Dentistry admitted its first class two years later, about the same time as the University Hospital registered its first patients.

Early in 1960, Medical Center faculty were planning the curriculum for the first medical school class, to be admitted that fall. Left to right are Dean William R. Willard, Joseph Parker, Edmund Pelligrino, and George Schwert.

Most students and faculty were more immediately affected by projects on other parts of the campus. New buildings went up from Euclid Avenue to Cooper Drive. Among them were three dormitories, Donovan, Holmes, and Blazer Halls; the Pharmacy Building on Washington Avenue; the Commerce and Law buildings; an addition to the Student Union; the King Alumni House; the Agricultural Science Center at Limestone and Cooper; the engineering tower, Anderson Hall; and the Chemistry-Physics Building. By the mid-1960s there was hardly room on the old campus for more buildings unless old ones were cleared away. The likeliest place for new growth was the Experiment Station Farm behind the Medical Center.

This was the most extensive and expensive building program in the university's history. As Donovan had done, President Dickey gave to Frank Peterson, vice-president for business administration, generous recognition for working out the arrangements for funding these enterprises.

During Dickey's administration the university moved toward more prosperous times than it had ever known, especially after the 3 percent sales tax of 1960 began to bear fruit. The budget for the biennium 1962-64, his last, was nearly $57 million, approaching three times his first and showing a proportionately greater growth than enrollment. The increase must of course be qualified by the greater costs of expanding graduate and professional education as compared with undergraduate education. The William Andrew Patterson School of Diplomacy and International Commerce, named for President Patterson's son, was established in 1960.

Amry Vandenbosch was part of the expansion of faculty and programs in the 1920s and remained until the 1960s. After heading the department of political science for thirty years, he was named first head of the Patterson School of Diplomacy, established in 1960. He enjoyed provoking discussions in small group meetings. In 1971 Vincent Davis became director. He is shown at left with a group planning a World Conference on Women. Many distinguished visitors have been invited to lecture and meet with students in the two-year master's degree program, including former President Gerald Ford and South African Bishop Desmond Tutu.

In 1962 the Medical Center was—for the time being—complete, and the first class, admitted two years before, could begin other phases of medical study: surgery and laboratory work, among many others.

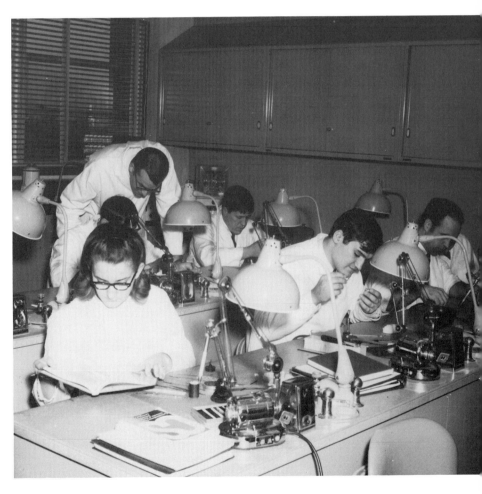

In 1964, administrators and faculty of the community colleges met at Spindletop Hall in Lexington to complete the working arrangements for the exciting new venture, created by a 1962 statute. The university community college system was then novel in the United States. It has worked well for a quarter of a century and has withstood occasional attempts to break it up.

Supported in part by income from President Patterson's bequest, the school admitted graduate students exclusively. Two years later the new school of architecture enrolled 178 students. These schools, like classes in the Medical Center, enriched the potential of the university but at the same time increased instructional costs considerably. Clearly, the university and its student body were changing.

The public, the General Assembly, and the governor's office were becoming more aware of the legitimate and increasing needs of the university, and the growing body of alumni helped promote that awareness. Alumni were organized in their own communities and in touch with campus affairs through the National Alumni Association; graduation did not sever ties with alma mater. Improved roads brought Lexington within easier reach of other parts of the state, and there was more at the university to interest citizens—

new buildings, new programs, athletics, and the Medical Center.

The year 1962 was a landmark in the university's efforts to reach out to the people of the state. On March 6 Governor Bert Combs signed a bill creating the University of Kentucky Community College System under the jurisdiction of the Board of Trustees and the president of the university. This was a mature form of the extension work that the university had been carrying on in one form or another for nearly half a century. The system would comprise existing centers in Covington, Ashland, Fort Knox, Cumberland, and Henderson; a new college already authorized at Elizabethtown; the ones a study commission recommended for Prestonsburg, Hopkinsville, Somerset, and the Blackey-Hazard area; and whatever others might be established later. These latter include Maysville, Madisonville, Paducah, Louisville, Lexington, and Owensboro. There are now fourteen in all. (The Fort Knox unit became a UK four-year resident instruction center in 1972, shortly after the College at Covington gave way to Northern Kentucky State College, newly created by the General Assembly.) Each community college is a part of the university, and its students are UK students, although locally enrolled in the Community College System rather than in the Lexington System. By 1983 the total enrollment of the Community College System, 24,059, for the first time exceeded that of the Lexington campus, 21,616. Enrollment in 1988 was 33,000.

In September 1962, Dickey announced his resignation, to take effect the following July. In May 1963, the faculty-trustee search committee was ready with a recommendation. Its chairman,

President Dickey and vice-president Leo M. Chamberlain lead the commencement procession of 1963, their last before retiring from their UK positions.

trustee Ralph Angelucci, prefaced the report with the gratifying observation that widespread recognition of the university's recent progress had made the committee's work easier.

The committee recommended and the board approved the appointment of John W. Oswald, a plant pathologist at the University of California, Berkeley, where twenty years before he had received his doctoral degree; he was now vice-president for administration. He was the first scientist to serve as president of UK and up to that time, except for McVey, the only outsider.

It quickly became clear that Oswald thought in big terms. The budget he submitted to Frankfort for the biennium 1964-66, contemplating an

John W. Oswald, UK's sixth president, is shown here surrounded by his family in 1963 as they took up residence in Maxwell Place. Oswald's five-year presidency, marked by campus growth and rapid academic change, overlapped the period of student protest, and his family's tenure of Maxwell Place was disturbed by campus demonstrations and student agitation.

The College of Architecture began as an engineering department but after four years separated to become a

school, with Charles P. Graves (above left) as dean and headquarters in Pence Hall. Today, with nearly

300 students, the college has long outgrown Pence and has plans to move to Scovell Hall in the near future.

increased enrollment and a larger emphasis on graduate study, provided for some three hundred new faculty positions in the total university. The resulting appropriation, though less than the university's request, was almost $20 million more than for the previous biennium.

Oswald's was an exciting administration. Not since McVey's first years had initiatives for change and enlargement come so numerously from the president. One of them improved faculty and staff benefits and the retirement system at a time when these were becoming important considerations in the employment of new faculty. Two others were controversial: When the criteria and procedures for faculty tenure were made more uniform, giving more weight to research, critics used the phrase "publish or perish" opprobriously; and rotation of deans and department heads, recommended by a faculty committee in Dickey's time but not acted on, was in-

stituted early in 1965 in a heavy-handed way that caused some unpleasantness.

Oswald was in a hurry to push toward what seemed an attainable goal of greatness, and the whole campus caught this sense of forward movement—trustees, students, and faculty. A revised calendar with August-December and January-May semesters exemplified the spirit of change; the faculty originated it and the students liked it. UK was a pioneer in the widespread changeover among American colleges.

On January 17, 1964, Oswald brought before the trustees the plans for filling in details of the 1962 statute creating the Community College System. Henceforth it would be one component of the university, the other being the research-oriented University System in Lexington. Mainly teaching institutions, community colleges would offer technical programs and two-year associate degree programs, with credits transferable to four-

Opened in October 1963, the Helen King Alumni House stands at Rose St. and Euclid Ave., waiting to welcome returning alumni for a casual visit or a festive occasion such as Homecoming. The late Helen King (right) was executive director of the National Alumni Association from 1946 through 1969. Alumni recall her fondly as someone who would always remember them when they visited campus.

The residence on Coldstream Farm was converted into a faculty club and named for James W. Carnahan, a prominent alumnus and benefactor of the university. Dedicated in 1958, it was replaced when the university acquired Spindletop Farm and its mansion a few years later. Carnahan House is now used as a conference center.

Frank Peterson spent 23 years as comptroller and vice-president for business affairs, managing the financial phases of all campus construction throughout the Donovan and Dickey administrations. Both presidents praised him for his business acumen and his resourcefulness in securing funds for the building programs. This 1964 studio portrait is appropriately superimposed on an aerial photograph of the campus, so many of whose buildings were erected under Peterson's superintendency.

The Donovan Scholars—persons over 65 who take university courses tuition-free—enjoy many recreational activities. Since many come from out of state, trips to points of interest in Kentucky are always popular. This group visiting the Capitol rotunda in Frankfort met with Lieutenant Governor (later Governor) Julian Carroll (right center), a UK alumnus. At left center is Earl Kaufman, who moved from the department of physical education to become first director of the program.

year institutions. Each college would have a local advisory board, and the system would be governed by the president and the Board of Trustees of the university.

The Community College System is one of UK's most successful enterprises. In 1964 it enrolled 2,876 students and twenty years later more than eight times as many. Occasional suggestions for breaking up this unusual arrangement have not been heard receptively, mainly because the system works.

Another successful innovation was the Herman L. Donovan Senior Citizens Fellowship Program, originally suggested by the former presi-

At age 102, the university library acquired its one millionth volume. In 1987—only 20 years later—the library celebrated the acquisition of its two millionth.

dent. Through the Donovan Program persons age sixty-five and over are admitted to classes free of tuition charges and can enter degree programs if they wish. The first Donovan Scholars appeared on campus in September 1964; today there are about five hundred, forming a group with a distinct identity. The program has received national attention. About this time too the university began to enter the broad field of studies on aging, and in 1970 the Center for Aging was established at the Medical Center. The Sanders-

Brown Research Center, a gift from Colonel Harland Sanders and John Y. Brown, Jr., in honor of Brown's father, a Lexington lawyer, is the focus of the work on aging; departments in other colleges share in the programs for senior citizens.

The mid-1960s continued the outburst of building activity that had marked the Dickey administration. Some of it provided expanded facilities for programs already on campus, such as the colleges of commerce, engineering, and law. One facility added something the campus

*The Centennial Ball in the Student Center
the night before Founders Day 1965 opened
the Centennial Year.*

had never had before, a separate building for
faculty offices, an eighteen-story tower domi-
nating the landscape of the old campus and visible from long distances.

Amid this rapid change, the university
community and many of the public looked
toward the celebration of a unique event. On
February 22, 1965, the university would be 100
years old. Committees went to work under the
general direction of the Centennial Committee
chaired by Thomas D. Clark, distinguished professor of history. If, as he wrote, "the close of a
century" is a "proper moment for stock taking,"

it is also a time to look ahead to "a more
enlightened future."

History was served by several publications.
Brief paperback profiles of some of the university's component colleges were handy references.
Charles G. Talbert's *The University of Kentucky:
The Maturing Years*, covering the Barker-McVey-
Donovan period, and Helen Irvin's *Hail Kentucky*, a short pictorial history of the university, were larger undertakings. An ambitious docu-
ment called *Beginning a Second Century*,
devoted to stock-taking and projections for the
future, was the work of a faculty-administration
committee.

Optimistic and self-congratulatory, the
Centennial dominated the campus for a year.
Some events, such as the grand ball to begin the
year, were specifically Centennial events. Others
that would have occurred anyway were gathered
into the celebration: the 1965 Homecoming, for
example, became Centennial Homecoming. The
Founders Day Convocation in the Coliseum on
February 22, 1965, marked the high point of the
year's observances. Eighty-five distinguished
alumni were recognized and an honorary degree
conferred upon President Lyndon Johnson. As the
year went on, the university received much
favorable attention nationally. The Association
of American University Presses assembled in
Lexington, and those in attendance took away
an impression of a campus on which good things
were happening.
One of these good things, the change of name
from University Faculty to University Faculty
Senate, was important because it meant an enlargement of the faculty's role in determining the
"broad academic policies" of the university.
Almost at once, in the fall of 1965, the Senate
adopted a new academic plan imposing a general
studies requirement for all baccalaureate degrees.

The high point of the Centennial was the Founders Day Convocation on February 22, 1965, at which 85 distinguished alumni were recognized and an honorary degree was conferred on President Lyndon Johnson. Johnson is shown with Kentuckian Whitney Young, Jr., president of the National Urban League. The Centennial closed a year later, when Arthur Goldberg, United States Ambassador to the United Nations, received an honorary degree and addressed the 1966 Founders Day Convocation. While ceremonies went on inside the Coliseum, demonstrations outside ushered in an era of student protests and demonstrations.

At the time of its completion in 1962, the Chemistry-Physics Building was the most ambitious piece of classroom-office construction the main campus had seen. Here, the atom-splitting accelerator is installed in the building's silo. It has served as the basis of much particle research.

(Modified, most recently in 1986, the original concept remains in effect.) The university also showed itself willing to expose to public view one of its shortcomings. Recalling that integration of athletics had been standing policy since 1963, the trustees curtly ordered full implementation of this policy in all sports.

The Centennial ended with another convocation on Founders Day, 1966. The events of that day also introduced a new era: as Arthur J. Goldberg, United States ambassador to the United Nations, was speaking in the Coliseum, student demonstrations were taking place outside. These were directed not against Goldberg personally but against the federal administration, which many people linked with the Vietnam War. They were the first of many demonstrations on campus in the next few years. Vietnam was not the only object of protests, but it was a major factor in creating a mood of protest that flourished among people of college age in collegiate settings. The spirit of anti-Vietnam dissent replaced the Centennial spirit at UK.

As the Centennial year ended, another spectacular building program was under way. On the sites of the old dorm (renamed White Hall), the old Patterson home, and the Carnegie Library, the eighteen-story faculty office tower and an adjoining classroom building were going up. East of the Medical Center rose an ambitious dormitory complex of two twenty-three-story towers surrounded by three-story buildings, the whole adjoining new playing fields. Preservationists protested mildly over demolitions on the old campus, and wits were unoriginally caustic about the perpendicular thrust of the new structures rising high over the landscape.

Of the same vintage as the engineering tower, the Law Building (above), to the southeast of Memorial Hall, and the Agricultural Science Center North (left), near the intersection of Limestone Street and Cooper Drive, speeded the migration of students and faculty from the old central campus. Impressive as they were when completed, these buildings were soon too small. The Law Building has since been enlarged to accommodate a larger enrollment, an expanded faculty, and a growing library. The agricultural complex at Cooper Drive now includes the Agricultural Science Center South, the new Agricultural Engineering Building, and the Tobacco Research Institute.

In early April 1968, students gathered in front of the Administration Building, where the Board of Trustees was meeting, as news spread of President Oswald's resignation. Oswald's appearance on the front steps pleased the students, with whom he was popular, but that popularity was held against him by some people. Even Oswald's popularity was insufficient to hold down the groundswell of student activism, fueled by the Vietnam War, that was to bring meetings, marches, and demonstrations to the once-placid UK campus, as to campuses all across America.

Amid all this building activity, pockets of discontent were appearing, especially among activist students and a few faculty. Stimulated by the anti-Vietnam War spirit, student demonstrations about a myriad of problems, some internal to the campus and others in the world outside, turned a segment of the public against the university. A local grand jury saw student complaint activities as evidence of the university's being out of harmony with "the desires of the Alumni and general public." Scruffy student dress styles raised many eyebrows. The meeting on campus in March 1968 of the unsavory-looking National Council of Students for Democratic Action (SDA) angered and disgusted many people.

How much all this influenced Oswald's thinking, when taken with his private reasons, cannot be determined, but in April 1968 he announced his resignation, effective September 1. Excitement over that announcement lessened the effect of his next one: the National Science Foundation had granted $974,000 for upgrading the mathematics department, enabling it to leap into the front ranks nationally. While students

Albert D. Kirwan had perhaps the most varied academic career of any UK president. A UK alumnus, he had coached football, been a distinguished member of the department of history, dean of men and dean of the Graduate School before being named interim president in 1968 while a successor to Oswald was sought. He was later named president retroactively.

demonstrated in support of Oswald, some of the public saw their support as a mark against him.

With no prospect of an early recommendation from the search committee, the board on July 19, 1968, appointed an interim president, Albert D. Kirwan of the history department. Besides having been football coach and dean of men, he had just returned to full-time teaching from the Graduate School deanship. Specializing and publishing in southern history, Kirwan was the most distinguished scholar who had ever occupied the president's office.

Widely known and respected, Kirwan was the ideal man to do what needed to be done at the time—improve relations with the public, with the alumni, and with Frankfort while maintaining the good will of both students and faculty. But first a brief settling-down period was needed. He and his wife Betty once again turned on the lights of Maxwell Place and opened the front door of the venerable house that had not been lived in recently. Traditions associated with Maxwell Place, which President and Mrs. McVey had made a focus of campus social life, were not lightly to be discarded and cried out to be revived, though students of the 1960s were too young to appreciate their significance.

One of Kirwan's first acts was to ask for reconsideration of plans for extending the library over against Maxwell Place. His suggested revision was obvious enough to cause wonder that it had not been the original expansion plan. Extension of the library northward recommended itself more strongly when the unlamented Splinter Hall performed its last service to the university by burning down.

The committee searching for a new president settled on a candidate by November and spent the winter in detailed negotiations in which Kirwan played an important part. Then, in April, a brief uproar occurred when four students were suspended for alleged drug infractions and, after hearings, not reinstated. Though the student code was revised to clarify such matters, some protesters remained unsatisfied with both the decision in the hearing and the revisions of the code.

The April 1969 demonstrations did not impede the presidential search, however, and on May 27 the trustees named Otis A. Singletary to

Otis and Gloria Singletary beam in May 1969, having just accepted the roles of president and first lady of the University of Kentucky. Given the restlessness of the UK campus, caught up in the agitations of the Vietnam War period, few would have predicted that the Singletary administration would last eighteen years, three times the average length of college presidencies in the United States. As the war wound down in the early 1970s, the university's troubles shifted to budgetary concerns.

In December 1969 the Board of Trustees met for the first time in its new room on the top floor of the Patterson Office Tower. By this time attendance at the open board meetings was large, and this room could accommodate more spectators than the old Board Room in the Administration Building.

the presidency. On a motion from A.B. Chandler, the board listed interim President Kirwan as seventh president of the university, testifying to his services in that extraordinarily important transition year.

Like his predecessor, Singletary was a historian and a publishing scholar. With a doctoral degree from Louisiana State University, he had joined the faculty of the University of Texas, Austin, in 1954, and soon students were acclaiming him as a teacher. Singletary later moved into administration at Texas and then went to the University of North Carolina, Greensboro, as chancellor. He served one year as director of the Job Corps and two years as vice-president of the American Council on Education before returning to Austin in 1968 as vice-chancellor for academic affairs, the position he was holding when he accepted Kentucky's offer. The university's constituency was impressed by Singletary's educational and administrative experience, especially since no previous UK president had such a broad background. The campus and the public were also pleased that President and Mrs. Singletary chose to live at Maxwell Place, where they could continue its tradition as a campus focal point, revived by the Kirwans.

Singletary came to UK at a time when a major problem involving higher education was confronting state government. The Council on

In the mid-1960s the original campus was extensively rebuilt. The Mathews Building (lower right in this aerial view), the Administration Building, Gillis Hall, and behind them Miller Hall and the engineering quadrangle, survived. The Commerce Building and Anderson Hall were completed by the time the old dorm, the Carnegie Library, and the old president's home were demolished to make way for Patterson Office Tower and the adjoining classroom building, White Hall. A few years later McLean Stadium would be demolished. The most striking of these new structures was the Office Tower, completed in 1968. Eighteen stories high and served by six elevators and two stairways, it has proved vulnerable to bomb threats, but the ultimate hazard—serious fire—has never struck.

During construction of Patterson Office Tower and White Hall Classroom Building, the site was surrounded by a plywood wall, which at once became a gigantic bulletin board for student notices and graffiti.

Public Higher Education had placed the future of the financially hard-pressed University of Louisville on the agendas of both the UK and U of L boards. Governor Louie Nunn, chairman of the UK board, urged the two presidents to prepare the way for bringing Louisville into the state system by placing both under a chancellor with a single governing board. When they could not reach agreement, the legislature resolved the matter by bringing U of L into the state system with a separate identity. It then created a new institution, Northern Kentucky State College, bringing to eight the total number of tax-supported institutions of higher education. Besides UK, U of L, and Northern, they included Eastern Kentucky, Kentucky State, Morehead State, Murray State, and Western Kentucky universities. Money to support these expanded state

obligations was found not by adequately increasing the total state appropriation but by taking funds from the appropriations for the six older institutions. So Singletary had hardly settled into the president's chair when he received the first of a series of financial shocks.

That same spring the university faced more problems on campus. A minority of activists among the student body were meeting and marching to protest various world problems as well as the "irrelevancy" of the university's curriculum to the needs of students. One student attempt to provide for "unmet needs" was the free university movement to organize "relevant" noncredit courses, as on other campuses. This activity lasted only about a year because, said the *Kentuckian*, the volunteer instructors could not "devote sufficient time to develop the program

Having called for a demonstration over student rights and the student code, Kernel *editor Guy Mendes had to announce that President Kirwan would not come out and speak at the assemblage. Sit-ins followed.*

fully." But there was a ready supply of people to address protest gatherings. In the background was always the anti-Vietnam War sentiment.

On May 4, 1970, as the school year moved to its close, the tragedy at Kent State University fanned student emotions red hot across the nation. The next day, May 5, UK's Board of Trustees sensed an ominous atmosphere as they assembled for their pre-commencement meeting. While students gathered outside, the board adopted more revisions of the student code. Calling these revisions "oppressive," the president of the Student Government Association, a nonvoting member of the board, said the code's inadequacy would provoke more demonstrations. He then announced a demonstration for the next day to protest the state of things at the university generally and the Kent State affair particularly. The board, in turn, promptly postponed commencement.

The next two days were the most dangerous the campus had ever known. Crowds of students and strangers drifted about, congregating finally in front of Barker Hall, the ROTC headquarters. Units of the National Guard, called out by the governor, reinforced armed riot police. The crowd

Following the shooting of students at Kent State University on May 4, 1970, campuses flared up across the nation. At UK, Governor Louie Nunn called out the National Guard. Tension was high, and the danger of some explosive incident was great, but the only serious occurrence was the loss of a frame building used by ROTC, which burned under suspicious circumstances.

UK was among the first universities to admit faculty and student members to the Board of Trustees, a practice now widely emulated. The president of the Student Government Association is by virtue of the office a student member; the first was Steve Cook, here being sworn in by Governor Louie B. Nunn in April 1968.

retired across Limestone Street without a confrontation, but during the night the Euclid Avenue classroom building, also used by the ROTC, burned for reasons never officially determined. The fire seemed to dismay everyone and helped calm the campus as the semester ended.

By the end of the summer this affair was only an unpleasant memory and on August 8 commencement took place peacefully. Then an ad hoc committee reported its recommendations for further revisions of the student code, and the trustees accepted them on August 13. The nonvoting student member responded, "We must resist. Gentlemen—we will resist." But although sporadic protests occurred, student unrest—more moderate than before the Kent State affair and

the end of the draft in 1972—wound down along with the Vietnam War.

Another reason for the subsidence of unrest was that recent structural and procedural changes within the university had given students and faculty larger roles in university affairs, making it easier to deal with campus grievances. For example, when student activists complained of underrepresentation in the University Senate, a new student trustee proposed an increase of student membership from eight to forty. A compromise of eighteen was agreed to. Subsequently, this student trustee proposed a new standing committee of the board, with himself as chairman, to study the code anew. That proposal failed.

Notables of many persuasions have been campus speakers, drawing crowds of the committed and the curious. John F. Kennedy brought his presidential campaign to UK in 1960. In the uneasy later years of the decade, two visitors at opposite ends of the ideological spectrum were Alabama politician George Wallace and trial lawyer William Kunstler.

The Medical Center, now on both sides of Rose Street, dominates the center of this 1986 aerial photo. The Roach Cancer Care Center is the triangular building, with Medical Plaza (housing outpatient facilities), the College of Pharmacy, and the College of Nursing across the street. The dorm complex, Seaton Sports Center, and Agricultural Science Center North are at right. Since this picture was taken, the hospital has continued to expand.

Throughout the disorders of this period, most students and faculty carried on with their learning, teaching, and research, and the state's flagship university, with its new president at the helm, sailed through the storms of the year into calmer waters.

Kentucky law stipulated that UK was "the only institution authorized to spend State General Fund appropriations on research and service programs of a statewide nature financed principally by state funds." That is one description of the "flagship" status the Council on Public Higher Education had bestowed on the university. External funding for research and other projects from grants and contracts administered by the Kentucky Research Foundation, plus corporate and private gifts through the Development Office, made up in part for continual budget deficiencies. The sums involved amounted to many millions of dollars.

The idea that a public university is a proper object of private and corporate giving and cannot depend entirely upon public funds has won acceptance among alumni and friends of the university to an extent beyond the expectations of only a few years ago. President Singletary made it one of his missions to emphasize this idea. How well he accomplished it can be seen in the annual reports of the Development Office and on the face of the campus.

The three big campus expansion projects under way in 1984 were made possible by gifts. The innovative Humanities Center on Maxwell Street came from the gift of John Gaines of Gainesway Farm, who has also been a supporter of the university's Art Museum. The Lucille Parker Markey Cancer Center adjoining the University Hospital came about through the foundation established by the will of the late Mrs. Markey of Calumet Farm. Dr. Ben F. Roach of Midway

The Lucille Parker Markey Cancer Center, shown below, comprises two buildings. The name of Dr. Ben F. Roach of Midway is given to the cancer care unit; the cancer research unit behind it is named for Dorothy Enslow Combs. George Bush, then vice-president of the United States, spoke at the dedication of the center in 1985. Here he is greeted by former Kentucky Governor Albert B. Chandler, a UK alumnus, in whose second administration the legislature appropriated the money to begin construction of the Medical Center named for him.

The Singletary Center for the Arts, on the former site of McLean Stadium, completed the conversion of the Rose and Euclid corner to an arts complex. The building includes an art museum, shown below with an expanding permanent collection. Its small recital hall and large concert hall host both student performances and guest artists of international stature. At right, professor of music Phillip W. Miller leads the university orchestra.

led the fund-raising efforts; major contributors included the Combs family of Spendthrift Farm, who donated in the name of the late Dorothy Enslow Combs. The Equine Research Center is the consequence of the initial gift of the late Maxwell H. Gluck and later gifts from other equine interests. All three projects originated from the generosity of people who, though not alumni, thought UK worthy of their confidence. All three projects now attract national and international attention and promise greater renown for the university.

To the casual observer, new buildings rather than research and program growth denote university expansion. So Stoll Field and McLean Stadium, abandoned after the 1972 football season in expectation that the next season would open in Commonwealth Stadium beyond Cooper Drive, were replaced by a second addition to the Student Center and by the long-awaited Center for the Arts, later named for Singletary. The new arts center, with recital and concert halls as well as an art museum, fulfilled the promise implied by the 1950 Fine Arts Building that the northeast corner of the campus would be devoted to the arts.

Except for construction of these buildings and of the Development Office building on Rose Street directly across from the arts complex, construction in the next years was concentrated in the vicinity of the Medical Center and related to the medical and biological sciences. Ever since the Medical Center opened in 1962, some construction project has been under way in the areas either adjacent to it or across Rose Street.

Farther to the southeast a tremendous expansion program resulted in the Seaton Center, a sports complex for track, baseball, and tennis, training facilities and practice fields for football, and intramural sports areas. These, together with the dorm complex built in the late 1960s, became a vast athletic and residential expanse covering the southeastern portion of the campus. Since then, building and development for recreational and sports purposes have gone on continually. Once Commonwealth Stadium was opened in 1973, and a little later Rupp Arena in the downtown Lexington Civic Center, intercollegiate athletics moved from the old campus except for swimming, gymnastics, women's basketball, and volleyball, still played in Memorial Coliseum. Today the name Avenue of Champions has only historic meaning. New champions, such as the football team of 1977 and the basketball team of 1977-78, have earned their laurels far away from the old campus. A very large part of

Registration at the Coliseum took patience and persistence. Since this picture was taken, pro- *cedures have changed to eliminate the long lines, but the process is still time consuming.*

student life—residential, athletic, and recreational—has departed from the vicinity of Euclid Avenue.

Physical changes on the 700-acre campus have affected profoundly the lives and movements of students, particularly their residential and recreational arrangements. While library facilities and most classrooms and laboratories for students in the nonprofessional schools remain between Washington and Euclid avenues, the old campus has had to surrender to the new south campus many of the activities that formerly took place there. Until early afternoon Mondays through Fridays, the patio in front of Patterson Office Tower is a crowded loitering and transit area; after that it is quiet. The Student Center is no longer the daytime social center that Mr.

The start of the school year for students living on campus or in town involves much effort and often vehicles larger than the family car. Today's student gear includes electronic and sports equipment. Books can come later.

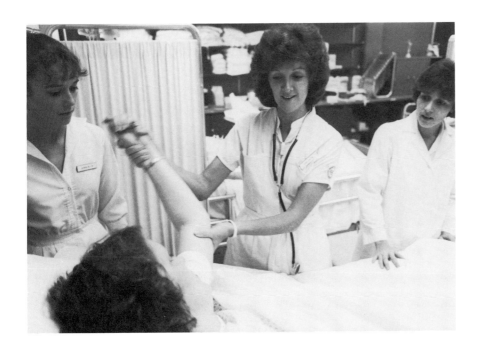

Nursing students at Hazard Community College get some hands-on instruction. One of fourteen such two-year institutions around the state, HCC specializes in work pertinent to the region. Community college students now outnumber those on the main UK campus.

An art student turns clay into a thing of beauty in the pottery studio. The artists' "garret" at UK is the Reynolds Building on South Broadway. A variety of studio courses is available, including painting, ceramics, sculpture, weaving, and photography. Campus galleries include one in the Fine Arts Building and another in the Student Center, in addition to those in town. A happy relationship exists with the Lexington arts community.

Creative genius means long hours of work for students in the College of Architecture. Preserving medieval traditions of masterwork, travel, and study abroad, the college enriches its students' education for entrance into what has become a controversial and prestigious profession. UK architecture students are making their marks in the profession.

In 1963, basic ROTC became optional rather than required for males. Women now take ROTC alongside their male counterparts. Congress in 1862, in requiring land-grant colleges to offer military science, could hardly have envisaged this development.

College life is filled with conferences.

Roberts's grill was in the 1940s and '50s. Alumni who were students in those days have something uniquely memorable to hold on to.

In the evenings the Student Center becomes busy with meetings or special events, and student cars replace faculty cars in its parking lot. In the Center for the Arts and up the hill are facilities for the lectures, concerts, and theater productions that so enrich students' collegiate experiences. These facilities also draw faculty, townspeople, and Donovan Scholars. "Celebrity" speakers and rock concerts, whether in the Coliseum, the Student Center ballroom, Memorial Hall, or Rupp Arena, attract large crowds of students.

The *Kentucky Kernel*, as always, trains its spotlight on the campus. To what extent it represents student opinion is arguable, but it is eagerly read. During the student discontents of the Vietnam period, it represented an activist persuasion, as did the yearbook, the *Kentuckian*. But the activists were a minority, and no one can say

At left, a proud moment as Willis K. Bright receives from President Oswald the Algernon Sydney Sullivan award for outstanding male graduate at the 1966 commencement.

what proportion of the nonactivists agreed with these publications and their editors. In 1969-70 the *Kentuckian* departed from the traditional yearbook style to concentrate on grievances, on and off campus. In a preface the editor assumed full responsibility for the contents: "The editorial comment, pictures and graphic design . . . are found not to be representative of student activities and therefore unacceptable for publication by the Director of Student Publications for the University." After quiet returned to the campus, the *Kentuckian* resumed its traditional yearbook role. At the same time the editorial voice of the *Kernel* became less strident. In 1971 it became independent, without university subsidy. Both publications are traditional parts of student life and record it for posterity.

Students have always been joiners, and their organizations have come and gone or endured through the student generations as they served temporary or lasting needs. During times of unrest, committees and organizations formed, enjoyed a headline or two, and then faded away with the passing interests that inspired them. The durable ones represent permanent campus urges.

The band, one of the oldest of student organizations, began as part of the military emphasis of earlier times. Now, reinforced by flagbearers and baton twirlers, it displays itself most prominently and colorfully at football games.

Organized cheering at games has died out; "cheerleaders" are less leaders of cheers than acrobats and performers. In earlier times chapel exercises were opportunities for the rehearsal of cheers and school songs. And in 1917 Professor Cotton Noe introduced at chapel two songs, "Alma Mater" and "Wildcats" (with its first line, "Hail, Hail, the Cats Are High," sung to an obvious tune). Neither song survived. Now the pep song is "On! On! U of K," and the current "Alma Mater" is "Hail Kentucky," both composed in the 1920s. Crowds no longer respond well to such songs, but those who know the words join in on "My Old Kentucky Home," which at football games has assumed almost the status of a school song.

A measure of changed student attitudes in the last twenty years was the abandonment after 1966 of the hallowed beauty contest. In 1969 a Miss UK was chosen, and there is annually a Homecoming Queen, but the criteria for selection are not those traditionally used in beauty contests.

There seem to be fewer displays of student high jinks than in olden times. Those that do oc-

ABOVE: *Fun is the order of the evening at the Phi Gamma Delta formal White Owl party in the early 1960s.*

OPPOSITE: *Before the system of ticket distribution was changed, basketball fans often camped out on the front lawn of Memorial Coliseum to be early in line for tickets.*

Much is expected of the wife of a university president, but Gloria Singletary (at right) went beyond the call of duty in passing out sandwiches among students lined up at the Coliseum for game tickets.

Staples of the college student diet.

The joys and frustrations of registration.

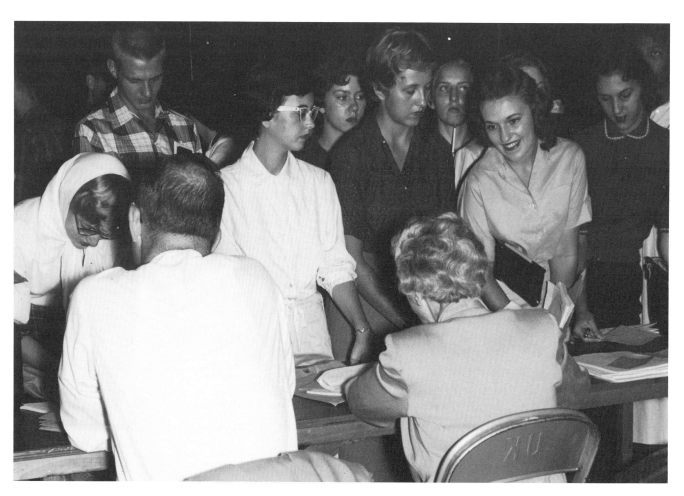

Even as McLean Stadium fell to the wrecker's ball in 1974, band director Harry Clarke put his students through their paces. What remains of Stoll Field still echoes to the sound of trumpets and drums and the sight of flagbearers and baton twirlers in the week before school begins each fall.

In this 1964 Guignol production of "Pygmalion," Margaret Sullivan, Phyllis Haddix, Bill Hayes, and Peggy Kelly converse in precise English accents.

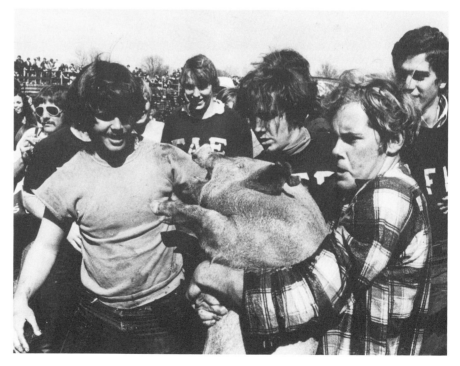

Races, pig wrestling, and a lot of horsing around make up the annual springtime ritual known as Little Kentucky Derby.

In sorority row off Columbia Avenue and Rose
Street, the actives of Alpha Gamma Delta gather
to welcome the 1969 pledges—the culmination of
the grueling ritual of rush week. Rushing for the

16 sororities and 22 fraternities is governed by
strict rules overseen by the offices of fraternity and
sorority advisors. The competition for pledges is
keen and therefore must be kept fair.

cur receive publicity only if criminal offenses are
involved. Spread about a larger area, college life
in modern times is less homogeneous than it was
on a more compact campus with a student body
mainly comprised of undergraduates.

Nurtured by the media, the traditional interest of the university community and the
public in the major sports continues with increasing vigor. The atmosphere at the games, however,

is not created by students because most tickets
go to the public.

For the past sixty years basketball has been one
of the university's most successful enterprises by
any measurement. Under coaches Adolph Rupp,
Joe B. Hall, who succeeded Rupp in 1972, and
Eddie Sutton, who came in 1985, basketball
never had a losing season until 1988-89; Rupp and
Hall each had one tie season. From 1957-58
through 1987-88 Kentucky won two NCAA
titles—making five in all—and Southeastern
Conference titles on the average every other year,

However prominent athletics may be, the Board of Directors of the Athletic Association is seldom photographed. The 1969 board shown here was transitional from the Kirwan to the Singletary administration. Kirwan is seated at left, with Singletary beside him; next is Harry Lancaster, director of athletics. Former Governor Chandler stands behind Singletary.

maintaining the reputation it had established as a premier basketball school.

Football has not fared so consistently well. In eight years under Blanton Collier the team had five winning and two losing seasons and one tied. His first season (1954) was his best, 7-3. Collier's record did not satisfy fans, and in 1962 Charles Bradshaw replaced him; of Bradshaw's seven seasons only 1965 was a winning one, 6-4. John Ray then compiled four losing seasons before Fran Curci replaced him in 1973 to inaugurate Commonwealth Stadium. Curci had three winning seasons and six losing ones, including his last four. His best years were outstanding, however: 1976 with a record of 9-3, including a victory over North Carolina in the Peach Bowl, and

1977 at 10-1; he had victories over Tennessee in both years. In fact, 1977-78, with the best football record since 1950 plus the 1978 NCAA basketball championship, was UK's second glory year.

Jerry Claiborne, who, like Bradshaw, had played under Bryant at Kentucky, returned to his alma mater in 1982, and by 1984, his third year, had put together the pieces for a 9-3 season, including a victory over Tennessee and a win over Wisconsin in the Hall of Fame Bowl. There is an old saying at Kentucky that a victory over Tennessee assures a coach's job. The record belies this: Bryant beat Tennessee only once in eight games, whereas Collier won five of eight and Claiborne, one in seven.

Dan Issel (below) played professional basketball for 15 years, retiring in 1985 from the Denver Nuggets to enter the horse business in Woodford County, Kentucky. As all-time leading scorer at UK, he racked up 2,138 points in his three varsity seasons; he is also well up on the list of all-time scorers among the pros.

After three seasons with UK in the mid-1960s, Pat Riley (above) went into pro basketball with San Diego, then moved to coaching. In 1981 he became head coach of the Los Angeles Lakers, with whom he has won four NBA championships, the latest in 1988.

Below: President Singletary congratulates Adolph Rupp on the achievements of his long and distinguished career in a ceremony marking the Baron of Basketball's retirement, March 6, 1972. Rupp would have preferred to stay on.

Joe B. Hall, head basketball coach from 1972 to 1985, seems satisfied with his team's performance—for the moment. During his tenure, Hall's teams compiled a record of 297 wins to 100 losses. His 1978 team beat Duke to win the NCAA championship, and his 1984 team made it to the semifinals.

Kyle Macy was named Southeastern Conference Athlete of the Year in 1980, his last UK season, and in 1986 he and Dan Issel were named to the 25-year all-SEC team. Macy went at once into professional basketball with the Phoenix Suns. After becoming a free agent, he played with the Chicago Bulls and Indiana Pacers.

The great expansion of professionalism after World War II offered many career opportunities for outstanding college athletes. George Blanda holds the record for longevity in pro football as a player—26 seasons beginning in 1949—and is the only former UK player in the Pro Football Hall of Fame. Two were elected to the Basketball Hall of Fame, Cliff Hagan and Frank Ramsey, along with Coach Rupp.

University athletes win fame and media attention never accorded to students who distinguish themselves in academic activities. Likewise, those who turn pro may, in brief careers, win national recognition never so quickly attained by

The year 1977-78 was UK's second glory year. The football team went 10-1, including a win over Tennessee, and the basketball team won the NCAA championship, UK's fifth.

Jim Master and Sam Bowie fight for a rebound against Illinois in the 1984 NCAA Regional. It was to be their last victory. A week later the Wildcats fell to the Georgetown Hoyas in a national semifinal game.

alumni in business or the other professions. If quick fame and fortune are criteria of distinction, then since World War II the athletic department has produced more distinguished alumni than any other academic unit in the university.

Organized intercollegiate competition in football began at State College only a decade after the college moved to its present site; and baseball, track, and basketball followed within another ten years—long before many present-day academic units appeared on campus or were even envisaged.

If custom establishes legitimacy, then administrators have to give attention to athletics as part of the university's responsibilities. After the Athletic Association was established at the end of World War II with the president as chairman of the board, having the power to appoint its members, no president thereafter could remain apart from either the athletic program or the people who conduct it. Monetary self-sufficiency (that is, independence from state appropriations) was a goal the association achieved at once, and the board is confident that revenues

Across the street from Memorial Coliseum, the house that Rupp built, stands Wildcat Lodge, the house that Joe B. Hall built. Intended as a posh dormitory for basketball players, it came under

NCAA criticism for giving UK an unfair recruiting advantage. The lodge is now under the supervision of the UK housing administration and is not restricted to basketball players.

will continue to sustain it, as they have for more than forty years.

Going with the trend nationally, UK has accepted that intercollegiate competition for women as well as men belongs in the university, and the burgeoning programs for both in the 1970s increased the prominence of athletic activities on campus by that much more. An old question, therefore, even more urgently demanded an answer: what is the proper place for athletics in institutions founded to provide academic education for the young? How much bigger can sports programs become and still be kept in balance with academics? By its nature, competition with other schools dictates that a program must become as big, or competitive, as

Eddie Sutton came to UK as head basketball coach in 1985 and resigned in March 1989 following an NCAA investigation of recruiting infractions. The NCAA allegations and final report did not mention Sutton by name and made no accusations against him. His UK teams compiled a four-year record of 88 wins and 42 losses; excluding the traumatic 1988-89 season, his record stands at 75-23.

Kenny Walker, who completed his spectacular career in 1986, pauses to concentrate before shooting a free throw. He was drafted by the NBA's New York Knickerbockers and remains with them.

Jeff Van Note won more fame in pro football than at UK. He joined Atlanta in 1969 and remained until 1986 as offensive center, winning All-Pro honors along the way. He was a striking example of durability and consistency as a player and of a much respected gentleman among his teammates.

Blanton Collier enjoys a victory ride in 1954 after a 14-13 win against arch-rival Tennessee. Collier compiled the best record against Tennessee of any coach in modern UK history. His teams won 5, lost 2, and tied 1.

A tense moment for Coach Jerry Claiborne. He came to UK in 1982 after successful careers at Virginia Tech and Maryland. His best year was his third, with a 9-3 record, including a victory over Tennessee. Otherwise his teams have not been consistent winners. But under Coach Claiborne the UK football program has won respect on the field and across the campus, with proper attention to its academic responsibilities. Few coaches command the respect that Claiborne enjoys.

Head football coach Fran Curci (1973-1981) urges on his players. Curci's first season inaugurated play in Commonwealth Stadium. His 1977 team, with a 10-1 record, was part of UK's second glory year.

those of its rivals. For this reason, control of an athletic program cannot be entirely within the university itself.

Recent evidence shows that at UK, greater attention to academics by those who control athletics makes for a healthier balance between the two. In that respect, Singletary reached a goal he set for the university when he became president. He did it by active leadership, though he was aware that in keeping close contact with athletics—which he frankly enjoyed—he would be seen as an athletics booster. Singletary took this risk to attain a wholesome, working balance that would allow athletics to flourish while the institution retained its academic self-respect.

(Text continues on page 207.)

With seats for 60,000, ample parking, and easy access from all directions, Commonwealth Stadium opened in 1973 for Fran Curci's first season as coach at UK.

Today's favorite style of attendance at football games is tailgating, by car, van, or motor home. Fans arrive early, sometimes the day before a game, to eat, drink, and be merry, and are in no hurry to leave afterward.

Jim Kovach (above), an outstanding student in his pre-med program and a star linebacker on the football team, received the B.S. on schedule in 1978, played pro football with the New Orleans Saints, and graduated from medical school in 1984. He is now James Joseph Kovach, M.D.

This photo of Jim McCollum, nose guard, was taken when he was a senior, 1972-73.

The Ervin J. Nutter Football Training Center, adjacent to the football practice fields and Shively Sports Center, is named for the alumnus who led the fund-raising effort. Nutter (B.S. 1943) twice served as chairman of the UK Development Council board. Seth Hancock of Claiborne Farm was another generous donor to the training center. The weight room, the showpiece of the building, resembles something out of science fiction.

Field hockey, long a staple of women's physical education, no longer exists in either physical education classes or intramural sports on the UK campus, in contrast to the Midwest and New England, where it has become a major fall intercollegiate sport.

Clifford Oldham Hagan was one of the stars of UK's undefeated 1953-54 basketball team and was voted All American. After playing for the St. Louis Hawks from 1956 to 1966, he coached the Dallas Chapparals and in 1972 returned to UK, becoming athletic director three years later. One of his responsibilities in that period was getting under way the women's athletic program. He resigned in 1988 during the NCAA investigation of the basketball program.

In 1924-25, women athletes of their own volition abolished intercollegiate athletics in favor of intramural games, which allowed many more to participate. Fifty years later the times favored women's intercollegiate athletics, and affirmative action demanded them. In 1974-75 UK renewed intercollegiate women's basketball and gymnastics; volleyball, swimming, golf, tennis, and track followed quickly.

After the men moved to Rupp Arena, Memorial Coliseum became the home of women's basketball and volleyball, the best that women could call their own of any school in the country. The Boone indoor tennis facility is shared by men and women, as will be the Lancaster Natatorium, both top of the line.

Wheelchair basketball for handicapped students is so well established that intercollegiate tournaments are held, this one at the Seaton Center in 1986.

From the looks on these baseball players' faces, there will be no joy at Shively Sports Center tonight. The center is named for Bernie Shively, who came to the university in 1927 and became athletic director in 1938. He died in 1967.

Just as schools and businesses interview graduating students for employment, so pro football teams conduct lively Pro Day "interviews" with aspiring UK players who have completed their eligibility. By 1987, 73 former UK players had played in the National Football League and 21 in the Canadian. Twelve had played in Super Bowls: Larry Seiple in three, Derrick Ramsey and Sam Ball in two each.

Flying through the air with the greatest of ease, the UK cheerleaders won the national championship in 1986 and 1987. They have long enjoyed national recognition, and their example has stimulated high school cheerleaders throughout Kentucky. Today's cheerleading is a far cry from the days when cheerleaders led organized school yells.

When President Singletary reorganized the higher administration of the university in 1982, the institution was divided into three administrative units. Peter Bosomworth (above left) became chancellor of the Medical Center, Art Gallaher (above right) became chancellor of the Lexington Campus, and Charles Wethington (above center) became chancellor of the Community College System. All retained their posts under President David Roselle, although Gallaher retired in the spring of 1989. In most administrative matters, the buck stops at their desks.

After moving with President Dickey from the College of Education to the office of presidential secretary, Anne Wilson continued in that protective role for the next three presidents, Oswald, Kirwan, and Singletary. She retired in 1979, having embodied the best tradition of that office: knowing how not to talk.

Of his generation or any other at UK, the most widely known faculty member was Thomas D. Clark (M.A. 1929). He joined the faculty in 1931, received his doctorate from Duke a year later, became head of the history department in 1944, retired in 1968, and then served for five years at Indiana University. A prolific scholar in Kentucky, southern, and western history, he was also a highly regarded teacher and a driving force in many UK developments, particularly relating to the library and the University Press.

Guy M. Davenport of the English Department is shown here with creative writing students. His literary criticism, short story writing, poetry, and translations from the Greek have earned him recognition in international circles.

At the 1973 commencement, Mike and Sheree Zalampas became the first husband and wife to receive doctorates at the same commencement—hers in musical arts, his in English and European history. Both teach at Jefferson Community College Southwest, where they have earned wide recognition for innovative team teaching techniques with computers. They received an award from the national community college organization in spring 1989.

Malcolm E. Jewell (below) is in the department of political science. His studies of voting behavior and of state legislatures are recognized nationally.

William Y. Adams (below right) is professor of anthropology. His archeological findings in the Nile Valley and the Sudan have won international acclaim.

Bernard Hennig (right) is acting director of graduate studies in the department of nutrition and food science, College of Home Economics. He is shown here with graduate students Manjushree Karkare and Angeline Alvaredo.

Dr. Mark Gillespie, professor of pharmacology, demonstrates a problem in drug administration for Bruce Bowdy, Trish Rippetoe, and Cheryl Haven.

Robert Straus (right) was one of the original group assembled to plan for the Medical Center and get it under way. He organized and was chairman of the innovative department of behavioral science, a model for subsequent changes in medical curricula. His scholarly reputation derives from researches in alcoholism and drug abuse.

William R. Markesbery is director of the Sanders-Brown Center on Aging. His researches in neurological diseases have brought recognition in the medical profession.

Joseph Kuc (above) is professor in the department of plant pathology. Of first importance to crop growers and to knowledge of plant disease resistance are his ground-breaking researches in plant immunization. His colleague Robert J. Shepherd (left) is the only Kentucky resident to win election to the National Academy of Science. His studies in DNA plant viruses are of special importance in tobacco and health research.

Thomas A. Chapman (below) teaches in the department of mathematics. His solutions to problems in geometric topology are hailed as major contributions to the field.

Virgil W. Hays of animal sciences is widely known for his work in animal nutrition. In 1978 he was chosen president of the American Society of Animal Science, and for 1989 he was president of the council for Agricultural Science and Technology.

Certain patterns have emerged among the careers of UK alumni during the past century. Up to about 1920 a large proportion of the distinguished alumni were engineering graduates who attained prominence either in the practice of their professions or in executive positions in industry. Technological changes in the field of communications after World War II changed traditional patterns, opening new branches that attracted many alumni. Since World War II professional athletics and high school, college, and professional coaching and sports administration have offered an enormously extended range of careers. During the same period, government service in enlarged bureaus at all levels appealed more than ever to university graduates from many fields of specialization. Those with backgrounds in law found many opportunities as elective or appointive officials.

There are many examples of well-known UK law graduates. Beginning with the first Chandler administration, 1935-39, all but three Kentucky governors have been UK alumni and all but two of these earned law degrees. In addition to A.B. Chandler and Virgil Chapman, two other alumni have been U.S. senators, and three of the four took law degrees.

Since the founding of the UK law school in 1908, many of its alumni have served on the federal, state, or local bench. Bert T. Combs, for example, became an appellate judge of the sixth U.S. Circuit Court; eight others have become federal district judges, all but one in the two Kentucky districts. (One of these judges is a UK alumnus but not a graduate of the law school.)

A law degree also prefaced the entry of some alumni into business careers: for example, Wendell Cherry, a founder and president of

W. Hugh Peal (B.A., 1922) was one of UK's ten Rhodes Scholars and went on to practice law in New York City. This picture was made in 1959, when he received an honorary degree from UK. He gave to the university his invaluable library of English literature of the Romantic period, along with manuscripts of the period. The gallery in King Library North is named for him.

Chloe Gifford (B.A. 1923, Ll.B. 1924) was
the first woman to graduate from the UK
law school.

William Nunn Lipscomb (B.S. 1941) was UK's second
Nobel laureate, awarded in chemistry in 1976.

Humana; the Webb brothers, Don and Dudley,
in development and construction; and John Y.
Brown, Jr., in Kentucky Fried Chicken. Tommy
Bell earned a law degree from UK but was more
widely known as a professional football referee
than as a practicing lawyer.

Some alumni achieved renown in ways out of
the ordinary. F. Story Musgrave as an astronaut,
Wendell Berry and Bobbie Ann Mason as writers,
and Chloe Gifford—the first woman graduate of
the UK law school and president of the General
Federation of Women's Clubs from 1958 to
1960—as a world figure.

Some eminent alumni of UK have won wide-

UK's College of Law has produced many fine lawyers and judges. Pictured here are a number of recent examples. Scott Reed (left, J.D. 1945) has served on the federal bench for the Eastern District of Kentucky since 1979. As a law student he was editor-in-chief of the Kentucky Law Journal and later taught for nearly a decade in the Law School. James Fleming Gordon (below left, Ll.B. 1941) served for the Western District of Kentucky from 1963 to 1985. After graduation in 1960, Henry Wilhoit (below center) practiced law in Grayson and was appointed to a federal judgeship for the Eastern District of Kentucky, where he continues to serve. He was president of the UK National Alumni Association in 1977. Harlan Hobart Grooms (below right, Ll.B. 1926) is the only UK-trained U.S. district judge appointed outside Kentucky, for the Northern District of Alabama in 1953.

The School of Journalism has produced two Pulitzer Prize winners, in addition to many other successful journalists. Don Whitehead (far left) studied in the department in the 1920s, writing sports for the Kernel, but left without taking a degree. Widely known as a correspondent, he won two Pulitzers for his reporting on the Korean War. John Ed Pearce (B.A. 1941, near left) went on to Harvard on a Nieman fellowship but returned to his native state to make his career, primarily with the Louisville Courier-Journal, *where he became one of the best known people in the Kentucky media world. In 1967 he received a Pulitzer for his writings on strip mining.*

ly respected prizes for achievements in the arts and sciences, thereby bringing distinction to the university as well. Two of these noted alumni—Thomas Hunt Morgan in medicine and William Nunn Lipscomb in chemistry—won Nobel Prizes. Two others—Don Whitehead and John Ed Pearce—won Pulitzer Prizes in journalism. Ten alumni have won Rhodes Scholarships for advanced study at Oxford University: Charles Howell Tandy (B.A. 1903); William Schacklett Hamilton (B.A. 1907); Reuben Thornton Taylor (B.A. 1914); John Henry Davis (B.A. 1920); W. Hugh Peal (B.A. 1922); Roscoe Cross (B.A. 1926); Samuel Shepard Jones (M.A. 1931); Elvis J. Stahr, Jr. (B.A. 1936); Floyd M. Cammack (B.A. 1954);

and Diogenes Allen (B.A. 1955). Most have gone on to distinguished careers.

Alumni returning to the campus have to look at it in new and much larger terms. Its physical size and bigger, more numerous buildings make the first impact on visitors. Enrollment on the Lexington campus totals more than 20,000, but because students are more widely dispersed and many are only part-time enrollees, the area may not seem any more crowded than formerly. The faculty, numbering about 1,000 (exclusive of the Medical Center

Elvis Stahr (left) fulfilled all the promise of a brilliant undergraduate career. After a Rhodes Scholarship to Oxford, he practiced law in New York City, returned to UK as dean of the College of Law, was Secretary of the Army, and ended his academic career as president of Indiana University, 1962-68. He then served as president of the National Audubon Society for a decade. He remained throughout a good friend of UK.

Wendell Berry (B.A. 1956, M.A. 1957) taught creative writing at UK for many years, dividing his time among farming in Henry County, writing and speaking out in environmental causes, and producing poetry, novels, and essays—for all of which he won national recognition. After a few years' hiatus, he recently returned to teaching at UK.

Rising rapidly in the literary world as a short story writer and novelist is Bobbie Ann Mason (B.A. 1962), far right.

Tommy Bell (B.S. 1948, Ll.B. 1950, left) officiated in the SEC and in 1962 became an NFL referee, a career that lasted 15 years and made Number 7 a television personality nationwide. Known for his decisive calls and distinctive style, Bell officiated in Super Bowls III and VII. He also practiced law in Lexington and served on the UK Board of Trustees.

Louis E. Hillenmeyer (B.A. 1907), who died in 1965, was a trustee for 18 years in the McVey administration, and his son Robert (B.S. 1943), served as an alumni trustee for 13 years in the administrations of Dickey, Oswald, Kirwan, and Singletary. They are the only father-son combination to have served on the board. Here Governor Edward Breathitt (right), another UK graduate, swears in Robert Hillenmeyer (center), along with another new board member, Hudson Milner.

William B. Sturgill (B.A. 1946, Ll.D. 1986) has been an exemplary supporter of UK. Generous in his monetary gifts, including funds for the Development Building on Rose Street, named for him, he has been generous also in giving of his time to the university. He served on the Board of Trustees from 1972 to 1984, serving as chairman for the last ten. He was reappointed to the Board in 1989. In addition he was chairman for a term of the Development Board. In his undergraduate career he lettered in basketball.

with about 500), are also more widely distributed; with varied schedules and more research activity, they may not be so visible on the campus, and they allocate their time differently.

Many changes are not outwardly visible. New fields of study have been introduced: computer science; black, women's, and Appalachian studies. In 1984 the university adopted a selective-admissions policy intended to improve the academic quality of the student body and to raise the retention rate of students. This policy and the 1986 revision of the general studies program

with accompanying curricular changes enable the faculty to assure a better quality of education for students.

Administrative changes are normally the preserve of the president and trustees. Unlike many presidents, Singletary did not begin with a wholesale reorganization of the administrative structure. Not until 1982 did a general revision take place, and it was the product of experience and mature consideration of local circumstances. Under the new arrangements, direct lines of responsibility lead to the president from three

Mitch McConnell (near left, J.D. 1967) has served since 1985 in the U.S. Senate. He is the fourth UK alumnus elected to the Senate, his predecessors being A.B. Chandler (Ll.B. 1924), who was also baseball commissioner and twice governor of Kentucky; Virgil Chapman (B.A. 1918), who was in the Senate from 1948 to 1951; and Walter D. Huddleston (far left, B.A. 1949), who served from 1973 to 1985.

Nearly all recent Kentucky governors earned degrees from the university: Albert Benjamin Chandler (Ll.B. 1924, pictured on pages 169 and 184), governor 1935-39 and 1955-59; Keen Johnson (B.A. 1922, opposite lower left), governor 1939-43; Bert T. Combs (Ll.B. 1937, opposite lower right), governor 1959-63 and U.S. Circuit Judge, 6th Judicial Circuit, 1967-70; Edward Thompson Breathitt, Jr. (B.S. 1948, Ll.B. 1950, pictured on page 212), governor 1963-67; Julian Morton Carroll (B.A. 1954, Ll.B. 1956, left), governor 1975-79; John Y. Brown, Jr. (B.A. 1957, Ll.B. 1961, below left), governor 1979-83; and Martha Layne Collins (B.S. 1959, below), governor 1983-87.

As a founder and president of Humana, Inc., Wendell Cherry (right, B.S. 1952, Ll.B. 1959) has been one of the most successful innovators in the field of health services. He is known also as a discriminating collector of art and a Louisville leader in patronage of the arts. He has done much for the revitalization of downtown Louisville and is a benefactor of the College of Law at UK.

Developers Donald and Dudley Webb (J.D. 1967 and 1968) changed the face and skyline of Lexington and other cities. Their Webb Companies is one of the country's largest development and construction companies, but their widespread interests do not diminish their concern for the well-being of UK.

After a varied career in the medical sciences as surgeon, physiologist, and biophysicist, Story Musgrave became an astronaut; in April 1983 he was mission specialist on the maiden voyage of the space shuttle Challenger, and in 1985 he returned to space, again on Challenger. His third space journey was scheduled for August 1989 aboard the shuttle Discovery. Musgrave's M.D. is from Columbia University; from UK he has a master's degree, 1966, and an honorary doctorate, 1984.

Early in its career, this double decker
traveled the streets of London's West End.
Now this gift from the UK Alumni Association, repainted blue, takes visitors around
the campus. Here Old Blue sits in front of
the flag plaza, another gift from alumni.

Hilary Boone (B.A. 1941), shown at right
presenting a gift to President Singletary, is a
Fayette County horseman who has been a
generous benefactor of his alma mater.
Mindful of his undergraduate captaincy of
the tennis team, Boone contributed largely
to the indoor tennis facility and even more
to the faculty club named for him.

We live in a truly revolutionary age much like the period 500 years ago when movable type introduced the first information explosion with printed books. UK entered the computer age in 1958 with an IBM 650, shown here with Carol Lotz, who was beginning her career with the computing center. The center began in the basement of McVey Hall, and now the building is known as the Center for Computational Sciences, housing hardware, classrooms, offices, and storage.

chancellors, of the Lexington System, the Community College System, and the Medical Center. These chancellors have enlarged functional responsibility and decisionmaking authority. The president, meanwhile, is less directly engaged than formerly in day-to-day administration and is freer to concern himself with the university at large and its far-flung constituencies.

The University of Kentucky will be 125 years old in 1990, having begun as the A&M College of an otherwise private, denominational university. Except for President McVey's early creative years and the seven years following the enactment of the 3 percent sales tax in 1960, the university throughout this century and a quarter has confronted financial privation. In 1968 the

Students can now be seen all over campus working at computers in offices, classrooms, and designated centers, and many have their own in their living quarters, while faculty and staff members have them on their desks or at home.

sales tax was raised to 5 percent. The additional revenue at that critical moment in the state's financial history enabled it and the university to preserve the gains of the abnormally lush times just ended but did not suffice to sustain the strong forward movement of the mid-1960s—a movement unprecedented in the university's history.

After 1970 the state and the university immediately resumed their normal courses, lacking funds to permit bold governmental and educational programs. Biennial budget increases, deriving mainly from natural growth in revenues coming from the established taxing system, were largely absorbed by increased costs of existing operations. Nevertheless, in 1970 the General Assembly, responding to political and regional pressures, added two more to the list of institutions of higher education dependent on public funds, and this without increasing the appropriation for higher education. Thus, a poor state, with a population of less than four million and with a history of inadequate support for education at all levels, found itself responsible for eight colleges and universities (all now titled universities), and within them two medical schools, two dental colleges, and three law schools, as well as many duplicated programs (in agriculture, for example).

Among the eight institutions, only the University of Kentucky is officially marked out to aspire to educational greatness. As the flagship univer-

The 3330 and (background) 3350 computers shown below were state of the art in the early 1980s. But in January 1988 they were replaced by the IBM 3090-300E supercomputer (left), purchased with a $5 million grant from the 1986 General Assembly and an additional $5 million from gifts, grants, and university funds. Among the wonders it performs are satellite connections with other supercomputers throughout the country, enabling the establishment of a national community of researchers.

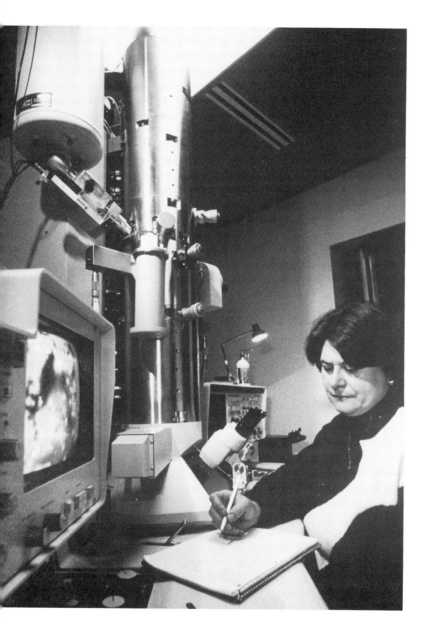

This electron microscope is central to an equine virus research project. Pat Van Meter assists in the project at the Gluck Equine Research Center.

sity in the system, it is the state's only complete university. Scholarly research bulks larger in its educational mission than in that of any other university; accordingly, graduate education is more prominent. The total educational endeavor of the University of Kentucky—undergraduate and graduate, professional, specialized, and community college—combine to make it the state's distinctive university, *the* state university of Kentucky.

The University of Kentucky aspires to a place in the educational world of the nation's great universities, those with comparable educational missions in which research is emphasized and expected. To compete in that world, a university needs a highly qualified faculty, the newest and best of research equipment, a large and well-developed library, and a bright, motivated undergraduate, graduate, and professional student body.

Nearly a century ago, one of UK's prized research tools was a homemade X-ray machine. Between the two world wars the newly acquired electron microscope was a sophisticated piece of equipment. With the Medical Center showing the way, after the 1960s came a myriad of instruments for research, teaching, and professional practice—including most recently the $10 million supercomputer that brings UK into the top ranks of computer research.

During this same century of development, the library's holdings have increased from a few thousand to two million items, the second million acquired in the short span of twenty years, primarily during the Singletary administration.

These are the expensive but necessary means for aiding the faculty to fulfill UK's role as the research university in Kentucky's system of public higher education. The university was established in the first place to teach the young,

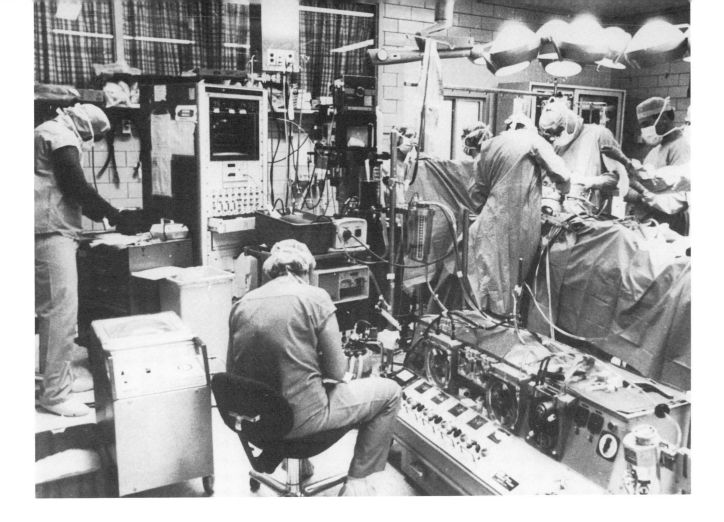

For all the drama this scene suggests, it is not a TV set but a scene in the Medical Center during open-heart surgery. In the foreground is a heart-lung machine monitored by a perfusionist.

and teaching remains one of its three chief functions. To satisfy this function means transmitting and perpetuating the accumulated learning of the past and disseminating the newest knowledge acquired by scholarly research at UK and elsewhere. Students are no longer predominantly the young of traditional college age. People of all ages come to the university as graduate and professional students, as extension enrollees, and as Donovan Scholars. Here the teaching and service functions of the university overlap.

The university received a research mandate from a statute of 1908 that assigned to its faculty the duty of seeking new knowledge by original scholarly research. For a generation the assignment was not accepted enthusiastically by many faculty members, and graduate education brought only a small number of students into the enterprise. But after World War II obedience to the research mandate became more widespread, and about 1960 it became virtually inescapable. A

(Text continues on page 230.)

UK's winning tradition in debate, its oldest form of intercollegiate competition, reached a climax in 1986 when David Brownell and Ouita Papka (second and third from right) won the National Debate Tournament. They are shown here with (left to right) Roger Solt, assistant debate coach; J.W. Patterson, debate coach; President Singletary; Harry Snyder, Council on Public Higher Education; and Governor Martha Layne Collins.

This intramural tug of war is a descendant of similar events across Clifton Pond, which replaced the annual flag rush in 1913.

Rugby football is a popular club sport at UK, played by both men and women. An ancestor of American football, rugby offers more continuous action.

With 14 Gaines Fellows (scholarship holders) in 1986, Professor Raymond Betts (seated, left), director of the UK Honors Program, and John Gaines, who endowed the Humanities Center on Maxwell Street, model their new scarves, which combine UK blue and white with the Gaines racing colors of green and red on black.

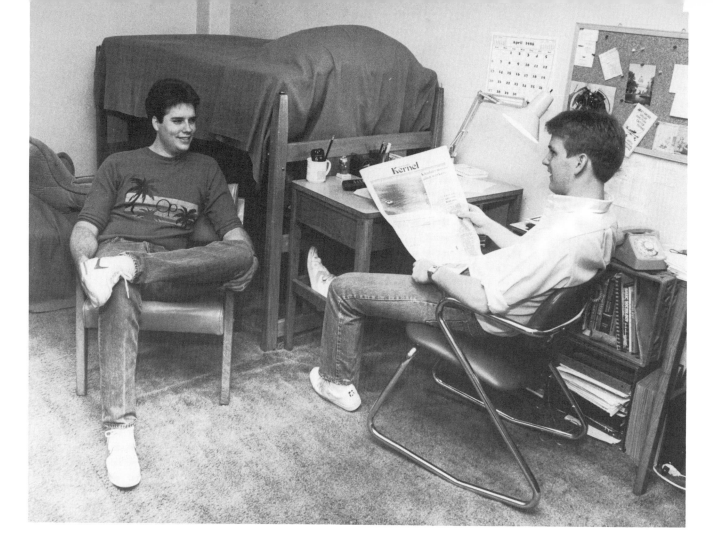

Dorm roommates take time out to catch up on campus news.

The rites and sights of spring at the Dorm Complex.

A student finds help at hand from a graduate assistant at King Library. The modern information explosion has revolutionized the search for information in rapidly expanding libraries.

The patio in front of Patterson Office Tower and adjoining White Hall Classroom Building is the place everyone crosses on the way from here to there. The fountain in its center is a popular meeting place, especially in summer.

How the Little Kentucky Derby has grown! It now takes place in the Commonwealth Stadium area. Here things are heating up for the great balloon race.

The popular choral group Black Voices performs on and off campus. It represents the kind of cultural programming the Minority Student Affairs office carries out. The office also offers educational and counseling services to minority students.

This column of two's holds onto their mortar boards in the wind as they approach the front entrance of Memorial Coliseum on their way to becoming UK alumni.

Out of the student movement of the 1960s arose concerns for many causes, some far away. Today's students manifest that same spirit for causes closer to home. Here Phi Kappa Tau fraternity holds a Mattress Marathon in April 1989 to raise money for the Children's Heart Fund.

When President Singletary told Hilary Boone of the need for a faculty club, Mr. Boone made a gift of a large portion of the construction costs. Opened in 1987 at Rose Street and Columbia Avenue, its location and facilities encourage the mix of faculty that Singletary had hoped it would provide. Busiest at lunchtime, the club offers amenities lacking elsewhere on the campus.

research ethos predominated on the campus, partly because it was soon built into the faculty promotion and tenure system. An unprecedented emphasis upon graduate education was also a powerful stimulus to research undertakings. By the 1960s the campus atmosphere had changed— though the change never stifled concern with the quality of undergraduate teaching; if anything, it elevated undergraduate understanding of the functions of a first-class university.

It is a tribute to the Singletary administration—given the history of state funding of the university and the experience of the period since that administration began—that UK has advanced as far as it has along the path toward greatness. Since 1970, with the squeeze to support two new universities, the state has provided only 40 percent of UK's operating budget instead of the traditional 60 percent. That proportion has remained, apparently fixed. Correspondingly, UK's portion of the state's outlay for higher education fell in 1970 from 60 to 40 percent, and that proportion has also become fixed.

That was all the more reason for the Singletary administration to emphasize so strongly the quest for funds from research grants and contracts and private benefactions. An increase in these revenues testifies to the quality of the faculty and of research equipment. The importance of these explains why competitive salaries for faculty are so crucial to forward movement of the university. When administrators talk about the salary scale while evaluating the adequacy of the biennial state appropriation, they are talking about a matter of pivotal importance. A decline in the quality and reputation of the faculty jeopardizes the university's ability to gain grants and contracts to support research.

The university development program seeks gifts to support additional needs and ambitions.

The program has come to be understood by private givers, individual and corporate, among whom many are alumni. Their gifts have a flexibility that research grants do not provide. In consequence of its success in these endeavors, UK has circumvented some of the restraints imposed by inadequate state appropriations and has continued to move toward a better and bigger future even if the pace is not as fast as desired.

In 1987 President Singletary, after eighteen years in office, handed to his successor a university much improved over the one he came to in 1969 and one that showed momentum. New programs and improved old ones offered better educational opportunities to students, and heightened admission requirements ensured a student body better qualified to benefit from those opportunities. New facilities, some directly related to new or improved programs, such as the Maxwell H. Gluck Equine Research Center and the Singletary Center for the Arts, were there to greet a new president. The supercomputer was on order and would be ready for installation the following year.

The search process for a successor to Singletary resulted in the appointment of mathematician David P. Roselle, provost of the Virginia Polytechnic Institute. Roselle's background included a doctorate from Duke and teaching experience at LSU and VPI. He took office on July 1, 1987, and quickly established rapport with the UK community. The university's larger constituency saw him as representing well the interests and values of the institution. His keen grasp of the essentials inspired confidence that the presidency was in strong and capable hands. Roselle shared the same aspirations for the university as

President David P. Roselle and board chairman Robert McCowan were all smiles after the new president's investiture on April 14, 1988, despite discouraging fiscal prospects for the university. Roselle wears the university seal on a medallion presented to him by his predecessor, Otis Singletary.

his precedessor and expressed confidence in the possibility of achieving them. UK had benefited from the unusual continuity of Singletary's eighteen-year administration, and the maintenance of that continuity would compensate for some of the adversities still facing the school.

The Roselles made many friends almost immediately upon arriving in Kentucky. They seemed especially to enjoy living at the traditional home of UK presidents, Maxwell Place.

Interest in robotics was stimulated by the location of a Toyota plant at Georgetown, a few miles from Lexington. The legislature appropriated $5 million toward the construction and equipment of this facility, which adjoins the engineering complex. When under way, the program will place UK in the forefront of robotics research.

Louise Roselle added her own special touch to the historic structure and welcomed hundreds of guests, including faculty, staff, and students.

During Roselle's first six months a sense of confidence in the future pervaded the campus, even though everyone was uneasily aware that an uncertain fiscal biennium was impending. A new governor, Wallace Wilkinson, took office in December 1987, and the legislature met in January 1988 to wrestle with a critical revenue problem. When Wilkinson, who had campaigned on a platform of no new taxes—an old state refrain—delivered his budget to the legislature, it confirmed the worst fears of many in higher education. The proposed budget provided for no increases in faculty and staff salaries and little additional help to a university seriously lagging behind its benchmark institutions. It was essentially a hold-the-line budget that appeared to shatter many hopes and prospects for a better future.

The disappointment was all the more acute in light of recent history. When UK celebrated its Centennial in 1965, there was optimistic talk about the beginning of a new century. The prevailing ethos at the university and even in Frankfort at the time was that the old criteria of educational normality would give way to new ones emphasizing growth and qualitative improvement, and that underlying these changes would be public acceptance of the need for adequate funding. The Centennial glow turned out to be only temporary, and soon traditional concepts of financial normality reasserted themselves. In the 1970s, the vision of a great state university as a statewide goal receded amid cries of "Go! Big Blue!" echoing from a new football stadium and a new basketball arena.

In response to Governor Wilkinson's funding proposal, President Roselle stumped the state, rallying alumni and friends of the university to

Beside the Faculty Club and opened soon after, the Mines and Mineral Resources Building demonstrates the university's enlarged emphasis on one of the state's major industries. Located within are the department of mining engineering, mines and mineral research, and the Kentucky Geological Survey.

ask their legislators to reconsider such a disastrous budget. Faculty and staff also traveled the state extensively to build grassroots support for the university's needs. To their credit, the legislators and the governor heard the rallying chorus and reacted with a higher education budget much better than the original proposal. The real problem, however, had not been faced—to provide adequate funding through increased state revenues. In short, higher taxes. It was a problem that would continue to nag the university and the commonwealth. Hence, when President Roselle was invested and the university seal hung around his neck on April 14, 1988, he had to speak somberly about the future. His address at the formal investiture ceremonies could not be a cheery message that all was well.

As budget problems lingered on, however, a presidency in its infancy was growing up quickly. It soon became apparent that the Roselle administration was going to be marked by an openness and vigor that would take the university's message to every corner of the state and to every department and employee on the campuses. It was a trait that particularly came into play when another problem presented itself—basketball.

On April 8 a telephone call to the president's office alerted the university—and very soon the entire nation—that the Wildcat basketball program was under investigation. The Los Angeles Daily News announced that it was going to print an article alleging that $1,000 had been sent by a UK assistant basketball coach to a Los Angeles recruit. Soon after the article appeared, the National Collegiate Athletic Association began an investigation.

The university cooperated with the NCAA, and the president appointed Lexington attorney James Park, Jr., to conduct the university's own investigation. The integrity of the institution was at stake, said President Roselle. The university would defend itself strenuously against any unfounded allegations but would also accept responsibility for any wrongdoings. Support for the university's announced goals of conducting a thorough investigation and maintaining an

Equine research, a traditional strength of the College of Agriculture, reached a high point with construction of this striking building, the Gluck Equine Research

Center, located between Limestone Street and Commonwealth Stadium and dedicated in 1987.

By popular demand, Charles Martin Newton came back to his alma mater in 1989 to inaugurate a new era of UK sports history. He had played basketball for UK, graduating in 1952, and went to Transylvania, where he coached until 1968, then moved on to Alabama and Vanderbilt. He took up his duties at UK after the 1988-89 basketball season, with responsibility for rebuilding the shattered program and repairing the damage done to UK's reputation in sports.

athletics program fully compliant with NCAA regulations was widespread across the state.

The following year was filled with news and rumors, often intertwined. While the NCAA conducted its investigation, the university's own inquiry went forward, its massive report being turned over to the Association in January 1989. Meanwhile, the basketball team played out its schedule under a heavier burden of uncertainty than any team in the university's history. The season record of 13-19 made it the first losing season in sixty-two years.

Other events added to the catalog of traumas. Athletic director Clifford O. Hagan resigned in November and was replaced by C.M. Newton. An alumnus and a player in the early 1950s, Newton had coached at Transylvania University and the University of Alabama, and was coach at Vanderbilt when he accepted the UK position. The clean sweep was completed when, after the 1988-89 season ended, head coach Eddie Sutton resigned and his entire staff followed suit.

A state of suspended animation followed. On April 22-23, the NCAA committee on infractions held hearings on the eighteen allegations of misconduct against UK and then retired to deliberate. A month later its decision was revealed. The university was placed on probation for three years, restricted to regular-season play for two years, banned from live television for one year, and limited to three recruits for each of the next two years. Two players could never again play for UK. In addition, the Southeastern Conference stripped UK of its 1988 regional title. The university accepted both decisions. Some fans thought the sanctions too severe, others were thankful they were less harsh than anticipated. Their chief consolation was that the Wildcat program would continue—crippled but alive.

Knowledge of the penalties removed the uncertainties that had handicapped the search for a new head coach, and on June 1, Rick Pitino,

June 1, 1989, will be remembered as the date when Rick Pitino signed on as UK's head basketball coach. Here he demonstrates his personal coaching style at Providence College, which he turned into a winner in two seasons. He had worked similar magic at Boston University and later with the New York Knicks. Wildcat fans hope his magnetism will restore UK's winning tradition.

coach of the NBA's New York Knickerbockers, signed a seven-year contract with UK. His job was defined as rebuilding the shattered basketball program while keeping it respectable—competitively respectable and operating within the regulations. Pitino's credentials were excellent. He had turned around losing teams at Boston University and Providence College with spectacular success before going to the Knicks, where he repeated his winning formula. His hiring was taken as a triumph for Newton and a vindication of President Roselle's reaction to the NCAA allegations. Fans' spirits revived. The thirteen-month ordeal was at last over. Better times surely lay ahead for the Wildcat basketball program, whose longstanding support was strong throughout the state and nation.

Although the basketball problem on occasion seemed to engulf the entire university, many other things were going on during the Roselle administration.

The supercomputer was installed and the university worked to push this important instructive tool as far down into the curriculum as it could. The facility placed UK among only a handful of universities in the nation with such sophisticated computing capacity.

Entering freshmen classes were continuing to improve every year under the selective admission policy begun in 1984. There were seventeen National Merit Scholars in the fall 1988 freshman class and a total of fifty-nine at the university in all classes. UK scholarships based on merit increased to more than a million dollars a year.

Enrollment in the community college system set records. In three years—from 1985 to 1988—enrollment increased 35 percent, to 33,000 students statewide in the fall of 1988. Total university enrollment—the Lexington campus, the Medical Center, and the community col-

Completing a year of astonishing changes in UK sports was the appointment on January 8, 1990, of Bill Curry as UK's head football coach. Curry, who replaced retiring coach Jerry Claiborne, had an outstanding record in pro football (Green Bay, Baltimore, Houston, and Los Angeles) before coaching at Georgia Tech (his alma mater) and most recently at Alabama. In 1989 he led his Alabama team to a 10-2-0 record, capped by a trip to the Sugar Bowl, and was named SEC coach of the year. By any measure, his appointment was a coup for Athletics Director C.M. Newton and a rallying point for UK football fans.

leges—reached an all-time record high of about 56,000 students. Applications to attend the university were also increasing each year. In 1988, UK received more than 11,000 applications for the 2,600 places in the freshman class.

Faculty members attracted record amounts in grants and contracts—$54.2 million in the 1987-88 fiscal year. Private gifts to the universi-

David and Louise Roselle meet with
students at Maxwell Place. The presidential
home was extensively refurbished in 1987
before the Roselles took up residence.

Robert E. Hemenway, former professor of
English at UK, then dean of Liberal Arts at
Oklahoma, returned to the university in
1989 as chancellor of the Lexington campus.
He is author of a prize-winning biography of
Zora Neale Hurston.

Charles T. Wethington, Jr., was named interim president of the university in
December 1989, after the resignation of
David Roselle. Wethington, who earned his
doctorate at UK, has been an administrator
in the Community College System for 22
years and its chancellor since 1982.

ty also set records. In 1988, new UK Fellows, those persons who give $10,000 or more to the university, numbered 210, a record for a single year. Total private giving each year was averaging about $18 million. A year into his administration President Roselle announced that the university was considering another major step in fundraising, its first-ever capital campaign.

Several new buildings were under construction—for robotics and manufacturing systems, agricultural engineering, and regulatory services, as well as expansion and renovation of hospital and Medical Center facilities. A master plan for the central core of the campus was unveiled, and work proceeded on a plan for the entire Lexington campus and the Medical Center, the work donated by an alumnus.

A free-tuition policy for employees was implemented as one of President Roselle's first employee-benefit initiatives, and in the first year some 800 employees took advantage of it. In only two years that number grew to nearly 1,500.

In 1987 came welcome news that the Carnegie Foundation for the Advancement of Education had named UK a research university of the First Class. The university thus became one of only forty-five public institutions in the nation with such a ranking.

Despite the basketball scandal and continuing budget concerns, then, Roselle's tenure at UK was marked by several promising steps aimed at moving the university toward increased national recognition for the quality of its scholarship, research, and graduates.

Then, on December 14, 1989, David Roselle announced his resignation to accept the presidency of the University of Delaware, saying that several factors had led to his decision, among them the long and difficult NCAA investigation of the basketball scandal and, more important, the discouraging long-term prospects for significantly increased funding for the university from the state. Two weeks after Roselle's resignation, the board of trustees chose as interim president Charles T. Wethington, Jr., chancellor for the UK Community College System, who had been one of the leading candidates for the presidency two and a half years earlier.

Thus with the University of Kentucky's 125th anniversary year dawned a new period in the history of the institution. The day after Roselle's announcement, Lexington Campus Chancellor Robert Hemenway wrote in a letter to faculty and staff, "Moments like these call forth the best in a university community. In our loss [of a president] comes the opportunity to show, with renewed vigor, that the University is committed to academic excellence, to serving Kentucky and the students of Kentucky. . . . That goal remains, and becomes a daily challenge. Let us focus on this challenge of the future as we move toward a new stage of the university's history."

His words echoed founder John Bowman's vision of greatness, articulated more than 100 years before: "We therefore want a University . . . giving education of the highest order to all classes. We want ample grounds and buildings and libraries, and apparatus, and museums and endowments, and prize-funds, and professors of great heads and hearts, men of faith and energy. Indeed we want everything which will make this institution eventually equal to any on this continent. Why should we not have them? I think we can."

Striving for greatness remains the continuing vision of the University of Kentucky.

Index